describe the crime, the weapon and the criminal and tell you where the criminal is hiding. But if he catches the criminal, he's lucky, if he doesn't, he's a dunce. If he gets promoted, he has political pull. If he doesn't he's a dullard.

The policeman must chase bum leads to a dead end and stake out ten nights to tag one witness who saw it happen, but refused to remember.

He runs files and writes reports until his eyes ache to build a case against some felon who will get dealt out by a shameless shamus or an honorable who isn't.

A policeman must be a minister, social worker, diplomat, tough guy and a gentleman. And of course, he will have to be a genius, for he will have to feed a family on a policeman's salary.

In the beginning

In 1899, 68-year-old, Henry Bliss, was helping a friend from a street car when he was struck by taxi driver, Jacob German, who was intoxicated. Bliss became the first person killed in an automobile accident, as well as the first person killed by a drunk driver. German was also the first person arrested for speeding. At the time there was no such charge as "DUI," since then it was not illegal to drink and drive.

Section I

Heroes in Blue

Officer Patrick "Doc" Sleffel

It was shortly after 2:00 AM, Christmas morning in the sleepy little town of Rome, Georgia. In Rome, the old saying, "they roll up the streets at night" accurately describes the quiet feeling that officers experience as they patrol the streets until early dawn. Doc was working sector 6 north. All was serene, no one was out, nothing going on at all. He had 4 hours left in his 10-hour shift. It started to snow lightly, and he was thinking, "This is one of those times you have to stop and enjoy the beauty of Gods nature." The streets were picturesque and the snow falling to blanket the streets can best be described as a Hallmark moment.

In the distance he saw a lone vehicle that was parked along the side of the road but looked out of place. To his surprise and disbelief, it appeared to be occupied. As he approached the vehicle, he was hoping that he wasn't stumbling upon a robbery-in-progress, not on Christmas!

He would soon learn the occupants in the car were a man, a woman and 3 children ages 10, 8 and 4. He wondered, "Run out of gas maybe?" He looked in the woman's red swollen eyes and noticed she had been crying.... a lot. The kids were crying and when the man finally looked up; Doc saw that he was crying as well. He asked him what was going on, now wondering if this was this a domestic? He told Doc they would be alright, and it was a long story. Doc responded with, "Well, I have all day, I need to know what is going on." The husband motioned to his wife and said, "you tell him." This whole family appeared to be in an emotionally hopeless state.

The woman got out of the car and proceeded to tell Doc that she was from Rome, but she moved away a few years ago and was married up north. She had been away for 11 years. Her parents had offered to let the family move in with them if she would consider "moving home." They lived with her parents for some time until they had "a huge blowout" and her parents told them all to leave.

Doc could not believe what he was hearing! How do parents put their daughter out of the house on Christmas morning, especially with children involved? What upset them? Was she being beat? Was she doing drugs? But, no, it was not any of the sort! She had a good husband. Unfortunately, he was out of work and the job market was tough. To make it worse, Rome had a reputation of "us" versus "them yankees."

Still, Doc had to make sure she was telling the truth. Officers learn that it's best to separate people and see if their stories differ. The man stepped out of the car to talk to Doc and broke down sobbing. He told Doc how he only had $5 dollars. His babies were cold, and he felt he didn't deserve to live.

DOC: God is watching Doc. Pull a miracle out of your ass buddy! No room at the inn. Make something incredible happen.

Part of his job as an officer is to keep close contact with the public. He met and grew to know many of the people he served in the community. He just happened to know the manager at the Ramada Inn. He knew that issue 1 was - shelter, get these people somewhere to stay. He told them to follow him but stay in the car until he comes to get them. He escorted the family to the Ramada and luck was with him! The guy he knew was working. Doc strolled in, smiled at the desk clerk and said, "Hi, pretty out this morning isn't it?"

"Hey, you checkin' up on me or just bored" he replied.

Doc told him he needed a pretty big favor. "Name it" the clerk responded. Doc told him he needed a room. "No," on second thought, Doc said, "Make that two adjoining rooms for maybe a week and, well I'm not going to pay for it." He looked at Doc like he was crazy and gave him the "come again" look.

Doc asked him if he was a Christian and he said "yes." He then told the clerk to look out front and proceeded to tell him the story. The worker yelled to Doc, "PUT OUT A FAMILY ON CHRISTMAS MORNING, you are damn right, oh sorry, you can have the rooms, we are empty now anyway."

Before Doc walked away, he again flashed his charming smile and asked, "by the way...kitchen open?" The clerk said, "it will be when we get that family settled." The family was soon registered, had their keys and got into their rooms. Doc describes them as awkward, proud people who were a little embarrassed about being needy and having to accept all of this help. These were good people. They weren't loafers looking for a free ride or a handout.

His attention then went to the children who were still crying. He bent down to talk with the middle child, a little girl, and told her not to cry. He said she doesn't have to stay in the car anymore and they are gonna get her whatever she wanted to eat. What this child would say in a few short words would reduce this 6'2" tall, 250 lb cop to a "blubbering crying mess." She said, "I'm crying cause now Santa won't know where to find us." Just as Doc was turning away from everyone so they didn't see that he was stating to cry, he turned directly facing two other cops. "Doc, what the hell?"

After Doc told them the story there were then three officers dressed in uniforms crying about Santa Claus. "Fuck this!" said one officer, "I got a number." Issue 2 was - Christmas for the children!

The officer worked special duty at a department store and called the owner, getting him out of bed. It was now between 3:30-4:00am. He told the store owner, he needed a favor! They needed a lot of toys, but they were not going to be able to pay for them.

In fact, your alarm will be going off in a few minutes and it will be me loading as many toys into my police car that will fit. The store owner simply responded by saying, "I've known you for years, I'm sure you have a good explanation. Merry Christmas!" and hung up.

It was time for some blue magic. Santa Claus was coming to town all right and in a big way! The second officer went with him, so there would be TWO cop cars full of toys! At this point only those three officers knew what was happening.

4

Doc went back inside, picked up the little girl and sat her on his knee. As the other children walked over, he told them he had a story for them. He whispered for the dad to open the door to the other room and keep an eye out. Doc proceeded to tell the little children that "Santa was a very, very smart guy and if they were really good children, he would know right where they were at." The children, wide-eyed and innocent, hoped against hope that this policeman, whom they had never laid an eye on before, actually did know Santa.

At this time, the family learned there were meals prepared for them. They had been driving around for hours hoping to find an answer to their problem, so the children hadn't eaten all day. After everyone was fed, Doc heard a click on his radio, letting him know "Santa" was ready to make his move.

"Hey," he called to the children, "Did you hear that?"

"What?" They asked. Doc clicked on his radio again. They were on car-to car which only transmits a few blocks.

He laughed inside as he heard the worst "ho-ho-ho" ever! He knew that God was making a difference in the lives of these children who were in such a sad situation that was not their fault. "Santa has a police radio" they asked in excitement! "Sure" said Doc. "We keep a look out for him."

Doc peeked into the next room he couldn't believe his eyes! "NEVER SEND 2 CRYING COPS SHOPPING!!" Piles of brightly wrapped Christmas presents awaited the children as there wasn't much space left to even sit down.

Doc stated, "this was the same year of the Rodney King situation and the police were catching hell from all sides." Not on this night! These men in blue were the shining stars for a family that was in great need of a Christmas miracle!

Everyone there that night was crying at the sight of these laughing smiling children who were ripping open boxes with a fury! The father dove at Doc, hugging him so hard he almost knocked the wind out of him. The dad told Doc "If anybody ever says anything bad about a cop again, I am going to kick their ass." "No, don't do that" Doc told him, "just pass on the love brother, just pass it on."

Doc was nearly out of breath and his uniform was wet from tears. He breathed a sigh of relief at being able to save this family. He explains that "no ribbon or commendation could equal the pure human emotion that I was lucky enough to experience."

He later learned that his impression about the family was right. The wife previously worked in a restaurant as a waitress and the husband did maintenance for them. He went on to find a job that paid twice what Doc made. They ended up staying at the hotel for 2 weeks. They later tried to give money to everybody involved that night, but nobody would take it.

DOC: "It's times like these that make all the bad you have to see worth it. Somewhere I think there is a woman that will never forget the night the police helped "find" Santa for her and her brothers. I will bet that for years to come there will be a family story about cops who made a difference!

One of the calls that Doc dreads the most are domestics. During one of these calls he met with a young couple that had a small child. When he arrived, the husband was outside and shaking with emotion.

Doc asked him what happened, he told him that he got a call about a domestic disturbance and asked if he hit his wife, though he did not appear to be the "type." He told Doc that he would never hit his wife, though he did yell a lot and was loud about it which is probably why the neighbors called the police. When Doc asked what the fighting was over, he was given the cliché answer...that he was working hard, and it should not be too much to expect the house to be clean when he came home. Doc ordered him not to move while he went inside to speak to his wife.

As he walked in, he saw the wife sitting on the couch and Doc noticed immediately one particular thing, the house was not really that unkempt. It probably just needed 5 minutes of light straightening up, nothing more than that. The wife gave Doc her version of the argument and he listened closely, trying to read between the lines.

Doc mentioned to her that he was also married and understood the problems that couples face. He went on to say that, even though her husband said the dispute was over housework he had a feeling that there was more going on and asked if she wanted to talk about it.

His keen officer instincts were right once more. They were a young couple, with a new baby and finances were tight. She went on to tell how the baby had been sick and needed to go to the hospital. She spent most of the grocery money on medicine and diapers. She knew her husband was working hard to make ends meet and it all came to a head when he arrived home after working 12 hours and there was not any food to eat. They were worried if they sought help, the state would take their baby away from them. Doc assured her that he wanted to help and that no one was going to take their baby. He then left the wife to go back outside to speak to the husband once more.

As he approached the father he simply said, "You know there is nothing wrong with being hungry. I know you are working hard and trying to make it for your family, believe me brother, I've been hungry. I have children and when they get sick, you really don't have many options."

The young man broke down and admitted to Doc that he was right, that is what the fight was over, and he was so sorry for taking it out on his wife. Doc told him that in his experience as a husband he learned that there is nothing like holding your wife and being man enough to say "I was wrong. It makes you MORE of a man, not less."

Once again Doc started to ponder over everyone that he knew in the community.... who can he call? Who can he ask for assistance? He remembered a lady in town named Penny who was the night manager at Hardees. Penny was a young black lady, and this was her first manager job. She confided in Doc that she was scared at night when it came time to close up. At that time, Rome was experiencing more than average robberies of fast food restaurants at closing time. Doc, always the knight in shining armor, assured her that if he was working her area and was not on a call, he would be glad to see to it that she got to her car safely. He gave Penny his pager number, so she could contact him when she was ready to leave. He didn't see it as anything special, only doing his job but she deeply appreciated it and he was about to learn just how much.

He told the family that he had a short-term solution. Penny once mentioned how much food they threw away every night. She said it was a pity that with so many hungry homeless people in the world that this good food was being tossed into the trash! In the next hour he became half cop/half delivery guy. He got them enough food for a few days and contacted a doctor from his church about the young family and their sick baby. He agreed to treat the baby at no expense to the family. Upon last contact with the family he learned that they had bought a nice car and were doing well. Penny always joked if he kept doing things like that, he was going to ruin his reputation with all the cop haters.

He said that one of the worst parts of his job was delivering bad news, especially on holidays. Among the more disheartening times were the three years in a row he had to deliver death notifications on Thanksgiving morning. Two of them involved the same father. Both of his boys had been driving too fast and died in car crashes. The first year was hard enough and the 2nd year when Doc pulled into his driveway the father just collapsed when he saw him.

Doc always felt that the saddest calls were always the ones that involve children. He believes that if a cop is not soft with children, then he is not real. He once put a man in jail for leaving horrific bloody marks of abuse on a child's back. It took him weeks to recover from the memories of that night. It broke his heart when he was putting him in the police car and the young girl broke loose from the officer who was tending to her and cried out "I am bad!" "I deserve it!" and screamed "I hate you" to Doc. She would be 20 years old now. He has wondered through the years if she ever thinks about him. Does she still hate him, or did she grow to understand why her daddy had to be arrested?

Many times, the press get in the way on police calls. One night Doc "helped " a media personality realize that sometimes it is best for people not to see what police officers see every day. He received a call to the state hospital where a man had been injured and there was extreme danger involved. The accident involved boilers and the fire department had to assemble a team with the knowledge and experience of working with them.

Since it also involved state property, they had to monitor the scene until a trooper could arrive. The injured man was working in "a pit" where there were exposed pipes. A tool of his had fallen from his tool belt and hit one of the pipes puncturing it. The steam was about 2000 degrees and under high pressure.

Doc couldn't get within 20 feet of the pit because his polyester uniform was actually melting from the steam being released. The man was killed instantly. The call went from a rescue to a recovery operation and then the media showed up. The reporter was a young lady who was determined to get the story.

Doc describes the reporter as being hardened and not interested in the tragedy of the wife who was contacted and standing close by. It was the smell from that night that he will never forget. Once the power of the steam had been turned off and the air cleared; the sight was unreal. It was almost like a nightmare being played out in front of him. In the background he could hear the reporter complaining about her rights as a member of the press. Doc was the senior officer on the scene and just could not take it anymore. He approached the reporter and shouted, "You want to see?" He grabbed her arm and escorted her to the pit in time to see the man being "recovered" by the fire department.

His eyelids were burned off, as were his fingers, lips and hair. He was swollen and not even human looking. There was a substance on the water that is something akin to what happens when you boil a hot dog. The reporter ran from his grip and began vomiting. She then got in her news van and left. He saw her several weeks later and she confided in him that "she had never had more respect for police and firefighters before this day." She also apologized for being pushy that day and admitted that she learned an important lesson. If a cop ever again tells her "you really don't want to see this" she was going to listen.

She and Doc have since become friends and he noticed that she frequently ended her broadcast with a statement about appreciating public servants. Yet, another woman influenced by this hero in blue!

During his years as a cop he saw the worst that life had to offer. He performed CPR on a child who was struck by a car and the child died in his arms. He comforted a dying man while life flight was being delayed from in climate weather; knowing he didn't have a chance of survival. He took a child abuser to jail for covering his little girl with cigarette burns. He answered a call from a family concerned about their mother who they were trying to reach, and she would not answer the phone. When he arrived at her home, he kicked in the door only to find the elderly mother dead on Christmas morning and then had to make THE phone call.

Injuries, such as bumps and bruises and even stitches are par for the course for the on-duty officer. In extreme cases an officer can suffer even more severe injuries. Doc was about to experience this first hand. One that would end his career and leave him fighting for his life!

It was during his night shift with Floyd County. Doc responded to a call to rescue a young woman who was beaten by her husband. The incident was in a remote area of the county and the department only had three cars on duty. He knew that he was taking a risk by responding alone. However, his duty to protect and serve his community is the inner force that made him an upstanding officer and it was that same force that told him he needed to respond immediately; he needed to save her. Doc was the type of officer who always put the safety of the citizens in his community first.

He was the first officer on the scene and learned the husband had fled when the neighbor hollered out that he had called the police. The woman was badly beaten and after he administered first aid, he called for an ambulance. He also contacted her family to inform them of what happened and summoned for them to come and take her out of there.

Doc stayed with her and waited for her family to arrive.

When her father saw his daughter with her swollen and blackened eyes, cuts and bruises and fat lip he was reduced to tears. His heart broke at the sight of the aftermath of what his daughter suffered. Before the family left the house, the father grabbed Doc's arm and with tears still in his eyes said, "please catch that son of a bitch." Doc also has a daughter and knew what that father must be thinking. The pain that a father would feel upon seeing his daughter beaten would bring on a flood of rage that is indescribable, to everyone else, except other fathers!

He could have been the "Joe Average" cop who files a report and lets the prosecutor take over from there but not Doc. As he puts it, he could not live with himself if he did not give 110% to his community. When he took the oath to "protect and serve" he took it to heart! His work as a police officer was not just a job; it was an honor. It was an honor to protect the citizens of the community and he was not about to let them down now.

He wanted to give this family the same respect that he would want to be given, had it been his daughter on the receiving end of that beating. He wasn't going to dishonor his profession and let this man go free from what he did. Though he could have done the "easy part" of the job he chose honor instead. He told himself, "you are a cop for God's sake, catch the bad guys!" He always believed that "criminals are criminals for a reason; they aren't really that bright and learn early to take advantage of others." They take the easy way out in life for they learn as early as high school that it is easier to slide by then have to work hard and actually apply themselves.

Doc learned early in his career that learning tactics makes a better officer and psychology plays an important part of this. He stated, "You learn to identify what people expect you to do and it can get you a slew of arrests by being where a criminal least expects you to be." Criminals think no police car = no police officer. He knew the man had run off into the woods. He also knew the man had to be watching and waiting for Doc to leave so it would be safe for him to resurface.

Doc made a scene leaving, making sure the man would have seen him leave. He turned on his lights and siren like he had just received an important call and peeled out of the driveway. Once he was two blocks away, he turned everything off and proceeded to sneak back to the house. He parked a few houses down in the darkness and walked back on foot. He went through backyards; jumping fences, to get a good view of where this guy was last seen. Doc then stood by the house and waited. He was only there a few minutes when out of the dark, the suspect came walking.

At this moment Doc still had the father in his mind's eye. He was thinking of how hurt the dad was seeing "his little girl" battered by this man. Through the blood and the emotional pain on her face he knew she would never be the same.

The suspect was cautious, looking everywhere he could to see if it was safe for him. Doc's position was perfect. He would have to pass by Doc to get to the house. He was three steps away and Doc stepped out and shouted "Floyd County Police, you are under arrest! Don't move!" Like so many others before him, the man turned and ran with Doc only a step behind. He ran back into the woods. Doc tackled him, and the fight began.

With 15 years of law enforcement behind him, this was the most violent fight Doc had been in so far. It became obvious that the man was on drugs due to the fact that Doc is a large man and though he was hitting him with everything he had, it was not affecting the suspect at all! Doc again called for backup ~ ETA 20 MINUTES!!

While Doc was fighting for his life the man was reaching for Doc's gun. His department had just switched from leather gear to web gear. The leather gives you the option of carrying what is called a level 3 holster. With that there is a trick to getting the gun to come out but not so with web gear. They had also switched from the Smith and Wesson's model 5906 9mm pistol to the glock model 22.40 cal pistol.

The key point here is with the smith, you "dump" the clip and the gun wont fire but with the glock, you still have a live handgun. The man was 20 years younger, faster, stronger

12

and a better fighter. They were throwing each other's bodies into the trees. Doc was losing the fight and now the suspect almost had his gun. He was able to wrestle the gun away from Doc and was trying to point it at the officer's head. Then it happened! Doc felt a sharp pain in his chest. He was sweating profusely, and weakness followed. He felt pain shooting up his left arm. He knew these symptoms well. He was having a heart attack in the middle of the fight! Doc jammed his hand in the "action" of the gun, so it would not fire but at this point he knew he was also passing out.

DOC: Your life really does flash before your eyes. Everything moved in slow motion. I wondered who was going to "make the call," who would tell my family I wasn't coming home......oh god, this will kill my dad....my wife....my kids.... when my baby girl was little I "pinky promised" her nobody would ever take her daddy from her. ...I had never broke a promise to her.

From what could only come from a higher power, Doc gained an incredible amount of strength and yelled "NO!" He regained control of his gun and wrestled the man to the ground and get him handcuffed. They fought for 20 solid minutes and Doc fought like a champion. A pro boxing match has 3-minute rounds, then a rest. The mixed martial arts world has the Ultimate Fighting Championship with 5-minute rounds, then a rest. When it was over all he could was just lay there and hold him down. Backup arrived, and Doc was taken to the hospital.

That night the department was supportive and concerned of his welfare. "Don't worry about a thing," is what they said to reassure him. Then they got the hospital bill ~ 6 figures! The cardiologist explained that the type of heart attack he suffered had nothing to do with plaque buildup or the like, it was the kind that is suffered by marathon runners and pro athletes.

Upon hearing this the department called Doc and explained that they were contesting the injury, siting it was not work related. Doc later learned that the department was self -insured so they saw the situation as being they can either toss out one used-up cop and save a quarter of a million dollars or do the right thing. Doc was forced to retire causing him to lose his house, his car and some of his sanity!

When Doc first decided to become a police officer; his biggest influences were his uncle and New York police officer, Frank Serpico. Doc believes that Mr. Serpico is what being a cop is all about today!

It was after seeing the movie, "Serpico" that he first knew that he wanted to be a cop. They have since become friends as well and the two keep in touch through phone calls and email. Which is an honor in its own right. It is not often that our mentors become our friends long after we achieve our goals.

Doc raves about the influence this man has had on his life and tells him often how much he appreciates his friendship. Two years ago, Doc's daughter suffered a stroke and nearly lost her life. He feels "Uncle Paco" was instrumental in her recovery. He would not let her give up and says he was nothing short of an angel. His courage continues to inspire Doc to this day.

Doc's road to law enforcement started in 1985, when he went to the Columbus Police Academy and graduated top of his class. He began his career at the Ohio, Columbus Police Department. Growing up, his family relocated often, and he grew to have a fondness for the Florida and Georgia states. In 1990 when a position opened for Georgia officers he relocated there and attended their Police Academy; again, graduating first of his class.

He went on to work for Georgia's Rome Police Department. Upon graduation he was voted "Best All Around Recruit" by the training staff and was honored with the opportunity of being the class speaker. His motivational speech for new recruits was given before department families and the media.

Shortly after arriving in Rome, Georgia he learned that his father suffered a heart attack. Doc took a leave from his job to move back to Ohio to aid in his recovery. Doc is an only child and his father raised him as a single parent; teaching him to always put his family first. He may have served his community tirelessly, but he has never let anything stand in the way of the love and protection he holds for his family. His father was his greatest role model and he credits his father for making him the man that he is today.

When he returned to Georgia, the Rome Police Department was in the midst of a hiring freeze and he went to work for Floyd County; it would be there that a fight with a spousal abuser caused a heart attack that brought Doc's career in law enforcement to a screeching halt!

Looking back, Doc explains he wouldn't change a thing that he did that night. He knows that he upheld the law and his honor is intact! He answered the question that is asked of all officers as a recruit, "Would you be willing to give your life for a fellow officer or citizen?" He answered "Yes," and stood by that promise as he nearly died on that night.

He did not think about his life. He thought about the young woman who was brutally attacked and what he can do to capture the suspect to protect her and the others in his community who slept safely in their bed that night.

In his career, Doc risked everything for Floyd County, Georgia. On this night, in a dark field, fighting an abuser, the stress finally broke him as he suffered a heart attack.

While Doc fought for his life in the midst of a call gone awry, he was still able to maintain control of the situation and prevent any other officer or citizen from being injured.

So why now, when he was down; would his boss then turn his back on him. One of their own, one of their bravest who fought for justice every day, was now in need of their help and his department abandoned him! To this day Doc continues to fight for his justice from Floyd County, Georgia.

During his career, Doc was awarded a commendation by the FBI Regional Task Force in Panama City, Florida for the capture of 3 serial bank robbers at gunpoint. As a stellar officer he was honored as the "Departmental Officer of the Month" four times and received numerous other commendations. He earned a certification as a Law Enforcement Officer in Florida and had one of his arrests reviewed and affirmed by the Supreme Court. Doc boasts, "it's a real honor to know you did your job perfectly in the eyes of the highest court!"

*If a teen stated that they wanted to follow in your chosen career path, what would be your advice for them?

DOC: Stay out of trouble. School! School! School! Honor above all!

This note was written by Doc's son. He is an image of his father.... from the inside out. He has emerged from his father's upbringing as a strong and just man. The love and admiration he has for his father is incomparable to what most family's experience.

MESSAGE FROM DOC'S SON

Where to begin...Maybe I'm just a little biased, but the most Loved and Respected individual in my entire world was hurt a few years back. I remember the day distinctly... The man that was my Father, my Mentor, my best friend lay in a hospital in Georgia, and there was nothing I could do but pray to God that his life would be spared. It was, and I thank God above every day for that. But take a look at the aftermath.

I take this whole situation extremely personally... Is there any other way for me to take it? I've watched the man that I strive every day of my life to live like, to be able to make him proud, struggle with the system. He almost gave his life doing what it is that he loved... Protecting the innocent... And he did... And he got hurt... And the people for whom he's served for the last 20 years have turned him away. How am I supposed to feel about this? You tell me...

I've watched his family grieve and almost fall apart... I've watched the future he was trying to build for himself crumble, I've watched the world he set up around him fall. But here's what hurts the most, friends. I've always said that if I can ever become one-tenth of the person that my father is, I'd be a good man.

What once was a strong, joy-filled, exuberant individual is dwindled down to a shell of his former self. His injury has hit closer to home that any of you might imagine. Now he's fighting for what's rightfully his and he's receiving resistance from all sides. It's just insult to permanent injury. Wake up, Floyd County.   -Patrick L. Sleffel IV

From the most tender side of Doc's life comes his daughter, Trish. She is not only the apple of her daddy's eye but he is in return the apple of her eye! Her dad is her true hero and the two have endured more together than life can put possibly put onto any father and daughter.

MESSAGE FROM DOC'S DAUGHTER

I am Pat's daughter...I have seen first and foremost what my father has gone through...this has affected him greatly in every sense...once a proud and true police officer is now reduced to a very unhappy man...ever since this has happened our family has lost everything...but the most important thing each other...I have always been daddy's little girl...and for those a@#holes that don't care about him almost being taken from me in the middle of a dark field...well...I just hope they never have to get a phone call from a fellow officer at 5am...Floyd county was at one time my home...where I knew most of my father's fellow officers as "uncles" and "aunts" and they are still aunts and uncles to me and I pray each night for their safe returns to each of their families...and hope that they never go through what I have seen my father go through...I just wish people would get more involved and reach out and help those EMTs, police officers, firefighters, that need it most...as a fellow emt...I have seen how all emergency service personnel have been treated...to my loving father...I love you more than words can say...we have beaten the odds once with GOD looking over you...we will beat Floyd county also. -Trish Sleffel (always daddy's girl)

FROM A FELLOW OFFICER

Pat, I was there the night you got hurt, I saw you lying in the back of the ambulance, and in the emergency room later. I drove your patrol car back to the station, because you were not able to, and I held on to all of your gear until you got out of intensive care at the hospital. I know what you went through on that night, but I can only imagine what you have been going through since. Floyd County P.D. has made it very clear for a long time that they couldn't care less for the officers who serve there, but the way you were treated is a new low even for them. As you know I have since severed my ties with F.C.P.D. I am still there for you bro, no matter what. I'll be praying for you, and I know you'll come out on top, just like always! Good luck, and God bless Brother!

(Name withheld for obvious reasons.)

"What do They Taste Like?" was inspirational to Doc as a police officer.

What Do They Taste Like?

The department was all astir, there was a lot of laughing and joking due to all the new officers, myself included, hitting the streets today for the first time. After months of seemingly endless amounts of classes, paperwork, and lectures we were finally done with the Police Academy and ready to join the ranks of our department. All you could see were rows of cadets with huge smiles and polished badges.

As we sat in the briefing room, we could barely sit still anxiously awaiting our turn to be introduced and given our beat assignment or, for the lay person, our own portion of the city to "serve and protect." It was then that he walked in. A statue of a man - 6 foot 3 and 230 pounds of solid muscle, he had black hair with highlights of gray and steely eyes that make you feel nervous even when he wasn't looking at you. He had a reputation for being the biggest and the smartest officer to ever work our fair city. He had been on the department for longer than anyone could remember, and those years of service had made him into somewhat of a legend. The new guys, or "rookies" as he called us, both respected and feared him.

When he spoke even, the most seasoned officers paid attention. It was almost a privilege when one the rookies got to be around when he would tell one of his police stories about the old days. But we knew our place and never interrupted for fear of being shooed away. He was respected and revered by all who knew him. After my first year on the department I still had never heard or saw him speak to any of the rookies for any length of time. When he did speak to them all he would say was, "So, you want to be a policeman, do you hero?" "I'll tell you what, when you can tell me what they taste like, then you can call yourself a real policeman." This particular phrase I had heard dozens of times. Me and my buddies all had bets about "what they taste like" actually referred to. Some believed it referred to the taste of your own blood after a hard fight. Others thought it referred to the taste of sweat after a long day's work.

Being on the department for a year, I thought I knew just about everyone and everything. So, one afternoon, I mustered up the courage and walked up to him. When he looked down at me, I said "You know, I think I've paid my dues." "I've been in plenty of fights, made dozens of arrests, and sweated my butt off just like everyone else." "So, what does that little saying of yours mean anyway?" With that, he merely stated, "Well, seeing as how you've said and done it all, you tell me what it means, hero." When I had no answer, he shook his head and snickered, "rookies," and walked away.

The next evening was to be the worst one to date. The night started out slow, but as the evening wore on, the calls became more frequent and dangerous. I made several small arrests and then had a real knock down drag out fight. However, I was able to make the arrest without hurting the suspect or myself.

After that, I was looking forward to just letting the shift wind down and getting home to my wife and daughter. I had just glanced at my watch and it was 11:55, five more minutes and I would be on my way to the house.

I don't know if it was fatigue or just my imagination, but as I drove down one of the streets on my beat, I thought I saw my daughter standing on someone's porch. I looked again but it was not my daughter as I had first thought but merely a small child about her age. She was probably only six or seven years old and dressed in an oversized shirt that hung to her feet. She was clutching an old rag doll in her arms that looked older than me. I immediately stopped my patrol car to see what she was doing outside her house at such an hour by herself.

When I approached, there seemed to be a sigh of relief on her face. I had to laugh to myself, thinking she sees the hero policeman come to save the day. I knelt at her side and asked what she was doing outside. She said, "My mommy and daddy just had a really big fight and now mommy won't wake up." My mind was reeling. Now what do I do? I instantly called for backup and ran to the nearest window. As I looked inside, I saw a man standing over a lady with his hands covered in blood, her blood. I kicked open the door, pushed the man aside and checked for a pulse, but unable to find one. I immediately cuffed the man and began doing CPR on the lady. It was then I heard a small voice from behind me, "Mr. Policeman, please make my mommy wake up." I continued to perform CPR until my backup and medics arrived, but they said it was too late. She was dead. I then looked at the man. He said, "I don't know what happened. She was yelling at me to stop drinking and go get a job and I had just had enough. I just shoved her, so she would leave me alone and she fell and hit her head."

As I walked the man out to the car in handcuffs, I again saw that little girl. In the five minutes that has passed, I went from hero to monster. Not only was I unable to wake up her mommy, but now I was taking daddy away too. Before I left the scene, I thought I would talk to the little girl. To say what, I don't know. Maybe just to tell her I was sorry about her mommy and daddy. But as I approached, she turned away and I knew it was useless and I would make it worse.

As I sat in the locker room at the station, I kept replaying the whole thing in my mind. Maybe if I would have been faster or done something different, just maybe that little girl would still have her mother. And even though it may sound selfish, I would still be the hero. It was then that I felt a large hand on my shoulder. I heard that all too familiar question again, "Well, hero, what do they taste like?" But before I could get mad or shout some sarcastic remark, I realized that all the pent-up emotions had flooded the surface and there was a steady stream of tears cascading down my face. It was at that moment that I realized what the answer to his question was. Tears.

With that, he began to walk away, but he stopped. "You know, there was nothing you could have done differently," he said. "Sometimes you can do everything right and still the outcome is the same. You may not be the hero you once thought you were, but now you ARE a police officer."

21

Sergeant Henry J. Ruiz

Prison Officer Michael "Mick" Jordan

Correction (Prison) Officers are often nicknamed "the forgotten cop," because they are not seen every day in the public eye. Their job is often not given the credit it is due. Make no mistake, their job is equally as dangerous as police officers, if not more. Those who attack Correction/Prison Officers are mainly inmates living with the "nothing to lose" mentality; so, in fact, the dangers extending from inside the prison walls are all too surreal.

Keep in mind, Correction Officers are surrounded by inmates who are charged with such brutal crimes as assault and murder. Many inmates act on the notion that since they are in jail for life anyway, it is no big deal for them to throw caution to the wind. Sergeant Henry Ruiz was reminded of this on November 14, 2000.

Henry: As a member of a six-man team of the Morris County Sheriff's Bureau of Corrections Emergency Response Team we were called away from their training to move an uncooperative inmate.

Upon entering the cell, the violent and mentally unstable inmate lunged at the officers and attempted to embed a weapon into one of their heads; the "shield man." They blocked the attack and while attempting to disarm the inmate the violent struggle continued.

Henry: The team's immediate action and skilled training, clearly prevented a potentially critical situation. Due to their action no staff member was injured. For these actions our team was honored with the Corrections USA National Silver Medal of Honor in Washington DC.

The Correction Officers brotherhood has no boundaries, their loyalty and dedication to each other extends around the world! In Ireland, Prison Officer Mick Jordan, is sweet and fun to be around while he's off duty. However, on duty he has been described as "Genghis Khan." In his line of work staying tough is a requirement for survival.

Mick also experienced, first hand, how the heated anger from the inmates can boil over to a life-or-death fight! Once while dealing with a group of inmates, he heard a call for back up come across his radio. Mick could hear the stress in the officer's voice. He raised the alarm box and raced to his location. It took Mick a few minutes to arrive to his aid, having to run through a maze of locked doors.

Mick: Due to the nature of the Seg unit it takes much longer for other staff to get to you.

His partner was in a scuffle with a prisoner who was armed with a "shiv" (homemade knife) and was trying to stab the officer. Mick and his partner were able to subdue the inmate; though it was a difficult struggle. Both officers were able to prevent themselves from being stabbed. They had him disarmed and pinned on the floor when the remaining officers arrived. Even then, there was still a lot of fight in the prisoner.

Mick: When the staff arrived, we must have looked a sight. Uniforms ripped, blood spattered (Not ours) and sweating heavily.

In 1989, Henry graduated from the New Jersey Military Academy in Sea Girt. He went on to serve in the United States Army where he was promoted to 2nd Lieutenant. In 1995 he was honorably discharged. He went on to attend William Patterson University as a Computer Science major. He was indecisive of whether to continue in that line of education. He was not sure if he wanted to spend his entire life behind a computer. His girlfriend, at the time, had a brother who was studying a career in law enforcement. It was after Henry talked to him about being a cop that he knew law enforcement was the avenue that he wanted to take. Today he credits George Baumann of the Freehold Police Department for being his biggest influence on making law enforcement his career. He earned his degree in Criminal Justice at Raritan Valley Community College.

He quickly rose through the ranks to Correctional Sergeant. He served as an acting supervisor for maximum- and minimum-security inmates, as well as, supervising and training subordinate staff and participating in various specialized teams. Those include Element Leader in the Emergency Response Team, Sheriff's Emergency Response Team and the Gang Intelligence Unit.

He had the honor to serve as the 3rd Vice-President with the New Jersey Policemen's Benevolent Association. He chaired the Correction Officers' Committee, Co-Chaired the New Delegate's Committee and was a Legislative Committee member. He was Web Administrator and Editor of "New Jersey's Finest" the PBA Newsletter. This is a union newspaper of the Police Benevolent Association.

He is currently a supervisor at the Morris County Correctional facility in New Jersey. While there he has served four terms as a State Delegate and two terms as President on the Union's Local #298. He assisted in the negotiation of several lucrative contracts while on their negotiations team. Henry also assisted in the establishment of the National Association of Police Organization's first Corrections Committee. He served as chairman for 2 years.

It was not until Mick was 30 years old that he chose a career in enforcement. In 1999 he went to work for the Irish Prison Service and continues there today. Once it is in you to protect and serve, no other career can be as satisfying.

Henry was assaulted numerous times while on duty. He knows the attacks can happen at any time and he has learned to constantly be on his guard. One angry dangerous inmate can spin his life around onto a new course that he may not survive on. Such as the time he was stopping an inmate from charging a fellow officer and without warning, the inmate punched him in the face.

In 2003, he endured another attack from a mentally insane inmate. Henry suffered facial injuries and had to be transported to the hospital. The hardest call he had to make in his career was when he had to call home to inform them that he was attacked and was on his way to the hospital. His youngest daughter was the only one home and upon hearing of her dad's injuries she melted into a puddle of tears.

As he reassured her that he was fine, his heart broke listening to her crying on the other end. He did not want her to hear the stress in his voice and had to pull the phone away as he choked back his own tears.

After the September 11th, Attack on America, Henry spent a day in Ground Zero delivering food and water to rescue workers. It truly is the day our country came together as one.

Henry: That day I saw the worst devastation I've ever seen in my life, but saw how people came together, and supported each other in the tragedy.

As many injuries that Mick has suffered it is when his comrades fall that hurts him the most. When a fellow officer was injured on duty Mick accompanied him in the ambulance and stayed by his side while he fought for his life. The officer was beaten so badly by inmates that they were unable to tell the extent of all of his injuries right away. En route to the hospital, the injured officer drifted in and out of consciousness. Mick was the one who later had to call the officer's parents to tell them that their son was suffering from life threatening injuries.

*If a teen stated that they wanted to follow in your chosen career path, what would be your advice for them?

Mick: I would tell them to leave it until their mid-twenties or older. This job is about common sense and life experience. And it makes you very cynical. I would tell them go live a little, travel and see the the big bad world for what it really is. And if the still want to join as they are a little older, I would tell them that the Job can either be one of the most enjoyable they will ever have or the worst depending on their personality.

Henry: That during our careers, the average correction officer will be assaulted at least four times. The stress of our jobs is so great that, on the average, we will not see our 59th birthdays. "We take the job because of the great retirement plan, and yet we may not live long enough to enjoy it." More than 33,000 of our co-workers were assaulted by inmates last year alone. Where we work, the AIDS/HIV rate is three times higher than the general population. Toxic cocktails comprised of urine, feces, blood, vomit, mucus and semen routinely are thrown at us.

Every year, we attend memorial services honoring the men and women who gave the ultimate sacrifice while doing a job few would dare to do. "Yet, to many we are guards, screws, hacks or turn-keys." Be prepared to work your next 10 to 13 Christmas, and New Year's. Forget about a 9 to 5, and weekend off. The first few times you'll love all the overtime, but eventually you'll dread it.

With all this in mind I've been a Correctional Officer for 19 years almost half of my life and have no plans on leaving until I retire at 25 years of service. My job is a love-hate thing. It all depends on what kind of a day I've had. Yet, I cannot imagine doing any other job, and many of the officers are like my extended family. A dysfunctional family, but family still. I would endanger my life for them and they would do the same for me.

Or do I tell how you change as a person? After working there long enough, most of if not all your friends are correctional officers. Your old friends don't understand you the way a CO does. When you go out for a beer after shift you say "No shop talk, but you know that is all you will be talking about is work. Yet when your loved ones ask you about work you have very little to say.

When you eat a a restaurant or go into a bar, you always have to sit with your back to the wall. As you have a conversation with your wife or girlfriend your eyes are always racing back and forth, scanning to see whats going on around you. As much as you try and leave work and home separate, there are times that invisible line gets crossed.

Behind the Walls......

*In the 1800's, the jails in small towns hired police officers, known as Night Watchmen to guard the prisoners. On March 15, 1808, George Workner of the Baltimore City Police Department became the first Night Watchman to be killed in the line of duty. He was stabbed to death during a jail break of nine inmates. Four of the prisoners were apprehended and sentenced to be hanged. Two days before the hanging they attempted to escape once more but were unsuccessful.

*On June 21, 1866, Jail Guard Uriah Gregory was attacked by two prisoners during an escape attempt. They struck Gregory over the head with a glass bottle. With blood streaming down his face, they forced Gregory into their cell. During the struggle they slammed the door on his hand causing extensive injuries. He developed a skin infection at the site of his wounds and died several days later. Uriah Gregory served with Nevada's Storey Sheriff's Department.

*William Bullard of the Missouri Department of Corrections was the first Correction Officer, working in a prison, to die in the line of duty. He was beaten to death on June 14, 1841 during a prison escape. One of the prisoners distracted him while another prisoner hit him in the back of the head with a hammer. He was then held down and beat to death.
*One of the most brutal deaths of a correction officer from the early days of American prisons was on May 1, 1833. Ezra Hoskins, a 66-year-old jail guard, who served with the Connecticut Department of Correction was murdered by inmates who were trying to escape. One of the inmates was

able to pick the lock of his cell with a dinner utensil and proceeded to open the cells of three more prisoners. The prisoners followed Hoskins on his rounds for some time before confronting him. Hoskins was deaf, so he did not hear the men behind him.

One of the inmates circled around and confronted him face-to-face while another prisoner attacked him from behind, striking him on the head with an iron bar. The four men surrounded the officer and beat on him until they were sure he was dead. A female prisoner noticed what was happening and hollered for the matron (female prison warden). The prisoners were captured and returned to their cell.

*The eldest correction officer to die in the line of duty was 70-year-old John Claussen. He was stabbed to death in the print shop of a Nebraska Penitentiary on April 16, 1954.

*On October 30, 1995, at the age of 19, Gregory Owen Cushing, of Indiana's LaGrange County Sheriff's Office, was the youngest Correction Officer killed in the line of duty. He died in an automobile accident while transporting an unruly inmate. The front of the squad car he was riding in struck the rear of a tractor trailer that was attempting to make a left-hand turn.

*The first female correction officer killed in the line of duty was Police Matron, Mary Davis. She was beaten to death by a female prisoner on May 11, 1924. The prisoner broke a pipe off of the sink and was using it to chip away at the wall. When Davis saw the water running out of the cell, she flung open the door to fix what she thought was a plumbing problem. The prisoner attacked Davis and beat her to death with a rock that she broke off of the wall. She served at the Wilmington Police Department in Delaware.

Correction Officers often find themselves battling inmates on the outside of prison, as well. That is, inmates who have been released from prison.

*Correction Officer Michael Sheehan of Westchester, New York was assaulted by a former inmate while leaving a restaurant on April 19, 2002. His injuries were so severe he cannot work in corrections again.

*On December 31, 1996, Washington DC Officer Amos Williams was robbed and murdered in a K-Mart parking lot. Witnesses say that when the robbers saw his Peace Officer ID, they shot him in the head. Williams served with the District of Columbia Department of Corrections.

*Tennessee Correction Officer, Deadrick Taylor was gunned down and murdered in front of his wife and child on April 19, 1996. Officer Taylor was shot by four gang members using assault rifles and .38 and .25 caliber pistols. Taylor was just returning home from work when he was ambushed by the gang for placing a fellow gang member on lock down status. Taylor served with the Shelby County Sheriff's Office in Tennessee.

"Ode to the Corrections Officer" was sent to Mick by a young Corrections Officer. To Mick, it sums up what they do perfectly.

Ode of the Corrections Officer

I walk down halls, of concrete and stairs.
Among the monsters, worse than nightmares.
With endless exposure to shanks and disease.
And to all of these felons, I still must say please.
The public is sheltered, kept safe from any harm.
While my heart is racing, I respond to the alarm.
A man is lying, face down on the floor.

Inmates are yelling, cut him some more.
With bare hands, and courage from above.
The disturbance is quelled without raising a glove.
We clear the compound and lock down the range.
For us inside, this is normal, not strange.
Behind these walls I've seen my share.
To the most horrible acts, I don't seem to care.
Violence and bloodshed are now part of my life.
I pray to God, don't let me take this home to my wife.
We spend our lives working in Hell.
Our stories are secret, we've no one to tell.
We serve in silence, no cheers or parades.
Yet the country is safer, by the service we made.

Correction Officer's Prayer

Lord I ask for courage
Courage to face and conquer my own fears...
Courage to take me where others will not go...
I ask for strength
Strength of body to protect others
and strength of spirit to lead others...
I ask for dedication
Dedication to my job, to do it well
Dedication to my community to keep it safe...
Give me Lord, concern for others who trust me
And compassion for those who need me...
And please Lord
Through it all
Be at my side

Deputy Stephen Ward

Lieutenant Jeff Cottingham

Four hours into his shift; Lieutenant Jeff Cottingham was

doing his nightly patrol when he noticed a small pickup truck parked on the side of the highway with the hood raised. He positioned his patrol car behind the truck and activated the emergency lights and spotlight to illuminate the interior of the vehicle. As he approached the truck, he noticed an elderly couple sitting quietly in the cab.

The couple planned on driving through the night to see their son who was in the hospital in another state, but their plans came to a halt when their truck broke down. Their son was scheduled for surgery the following morning and they needed to be there. They were justifiably distraught as they had lost power in their vehicle due to a faulty battery. Jeff offered to contact friends or family in the area that could assist them but there was no one and the car part stores were closed. This is one of those times when an officer's job is that of 'problem solver.' They have to think quickly. *Who do they know? What connections do they have?*

Jeff knew he had to save them from a hopeless situation. This sweet couple was appreciative of his concern and told him not to worry about them. They planned on sitting quietly in their vehicle on the side of the road until morning when the parts stores opened. The compassionate part of him could not fathom leaving this couple on the side of the road.

Jeff: Every so often an officer gets a chance to do that which truly typifies the term civil service. This was one of those moments for me. I had the chance to help these people and I was determined to do so.

He knew a part-time dispatcher that managed a local parts store, so he decided to take a chance and drove to his home. It was 2 AM, Jeff woke him from a sound sleep and explained the situation. After pleading with the him for a favor, he agreed to assist Jeff and the couple. Together they opened the parts store and Jeff purchased the battery that the couple needed. When Jeff returned, he found the woman in tears. Though she was appreciative to Jeff; she explained that they lived on a fixed income and simply did not have the means to pay for any parts or repairs. He took her by the hand, assured her that she was going to see her son and went on to explain that they need not worry about the cost. Her hand began to tremble as her eyes once again filled with tears. He was humbled by the opportunity to give of himself and was swept over with a feeling of accomplishment as he replaced the battery and closed the hood.

As he watched the couple drive off into the darkness he stood there in the silence of the night. He composed himself and went back to duty. Though the couple felt they had been saved by an angel in blue, to him it was another part of connecting with the community. It felt great to do something good for someone else and expect nothing in return.

A month later he walked into work and there was a small envelope laying on the desk addressed to him. He was, once more, moved by the events of that night as he read the thoughtful words from the elderly woman as she expressed her deepest gratitude for his kindness.

Jeff was 23 years old when he was first encouraged (by an older cousin) to pursue a career in law enforcement. He began his career in 1998 as a Patrol Officer for New Boston Police Department in Texas. He credits his experience in the small department of New Boston with enabling him to gain the knowledge and skills needed in his career.

Jeff: Each officer was responsible for working their own cases. If I received a call of a burglary already occurred then I took the report, processed the scene, gathered all pertinent information, interviewed witnesses and suspects, made arrests or secured warrants, processed arrestees, and developed the case file for the Prosecutors office. This broad sweep of duties allowed me to grow in several areas and gave me a keen understanding of the importance of details and thoroughness of the initial officers.

At NBPD there were only 9 officers, including the Chief of Police, which often lead to the problem of most shifts being covered by only one officer. Cottingham explained, "It was crucial that they remained on guard at all times." They were expected to do preventive patrol, which meant increasing patrol for problem areas and investigating anything out of the ordinary, such as, open doors, lights on, and open windows. They also served as Community Oriented Officers in the different neighborhoods and housing projects; building a bond between the community and the officers.

Jeff: I never wanted fame or fortune I simply wanted to know that when my family had laid their heads to a pillow each night there would be someone to stand between them and evil. My reward is bringing comfort or peace to a life that no longer possesses either.

After seven years with New Boston Police he left to join Texarkana College Police Department. Longtime friend, Deputy Stephen Ward, also served alongside Jeff at Texarkana PD. Stephen began his career with the Law Enforcement Explorer Program at the Texarkana, Arkansas Police Department. For six years he worked with the Public Relations Division and had several opportunities to ride along with the officers. He credits them with educating him on the proper ways to handle the public. They taught him to be understanding and compassionate.

It was until seven years later that he would join the Texarkana College Police Department. He started as a Patrol Officer and within several months he was promoted to Sergeant due to his experience and level of college education. This is the position he was most fond of; the position that molded him into the officer that he is today.

One reason Stephen enjoyed the Texarkana College PD is that Jeff (the Lieutenant) and the Captain were his best friends. In 1998 the three men went through the police academy together and ironically (seven years later) they all ended up in the same police department.

Stephen: Secondly, I had the opportunity to help my friends create a department of our own. We constantly strive to bring a more professional, compassionate department to our school. We want to be able to give better service and a safer environment for our students, staff and faculty. Most importantly, I want to be able to give back to my community and help others in their lives.

Today Stephen is a Deputy Sheriff with the Miller County Sheriff's Office where he holds the rank of Detective. He is also a certified Police Officer in Arkansas and Texas.

Stephen was put to a true test of any officer when he had to answer a call regarding a fellow officer. The man's wife of 15 years left him. He was distraught and believed his life was over and as the days went on it was becoming more difficult for him to bear the pain. There was an emptiness inside him that left a sting of betrayal. Such a state can leave someone feeling as if they are swimming in a pool of depression. Divorce is one of the most trying experiences a person can go through and police officers are no strangers to that pain.

When the distress call came across the radio, Stephen proceeded to the officer's home. Upon his arrival he was told that he had already left the house and was armed with his service weapon. It was a heart wrenching moment for both officers involved and would soon come to a head on the college campus as they faced each other.

Stephen: I received a call from a security officer at the college, stating that the officer in question was in an unused area on the college. I proceeded to that location where I had to remove my best friend at gunpoint. Unfortunately, I was ready to use deadly force if necessary, to protect the community, in which I served, from my friend. I was able to talk this officer down and place him into protective custody. City Officers were able to subdue the situation. He eventually returned to duty but hasn't been the same since that incident that afternoon.

It was the calls they ran early in their careers that had the biggest impact on Jeff and Stephen. In Jeff's first year he was reminded that there was one part of the public who looked up to him most for assurance: the children. He was a rookie officer and was experiencing the darkest sides of how people lived their lives. He often found himself re-evaluating his view of the public in general. Drugs and alcohol have destroyed lives and led the sweetest most gentle people to become cruel, heartless and desensitized. Alcohol drove people to abuse children and rob and degrade their fellow human beings. How is it that people could choose to live their lives in this manner? Why do they want to live in such sadness and despair? These questions haunted his days.

Jeff: I was constantly amazed at the conditions that people would allow themselves to exist in. I say exist because they were not living but simply existing.

This was never more evident than the day he answered a domestic disturbance in progress call. When he arrived, he noticed beer cans strewn across the yard of a dilapidated house. He approached with caution and made contact with the mother; a young woman with the sadness of the world in her eyes. She had the beaten look of life's toll. They talked briefly before he entered the home.

Jeff: I was immediately hit by a horrendous smell. I scanned the living room and saw two small children sitting on the floor. These children had dirty faces and looked as if they had not been bathed in several days. They were unclothed except for a diaper that was way beyond its intended capacity. They had sores on their legs and what appeared to be severe diaper rash. The children were crying and picking at what appeared to be an old half eaten hamburger that was lying on the floor. There were numerous empty beer cans on the make shift coffee table and an intoxicated male lying on a sofa smoking a cigarette and drinking a beer oblivious to my presence as he was caught up in the frivolity of the professional wrestling on the television.

Jeff inspected the remainder of the home and found each room to be in worse condition than the one before it. He noticed, an extreme absence of food in the refrigerator and several bottles of prescription medication lying on a low shelf, well within reach of the children. As he re-entered the living room the oldest daughter, who was the tender age of three, wrapped around his leg and clung hard onto him.

The father went into a drunken tirade that startled the little girl as she showed obvious fear of him. She raised her arms in the air at Jeff, who thought it was sad that this sweet young girl would seek protection in the arms of a stranger. For her safety, he diverted her into another direction, as the father continued to grow belligerent and hostile. There was a brief struggle and Jeff placed him under arrest.

Jeff then contacted Child Protective Services and sat on the front porch while he awaited their arrival. Once again, the little girl approached the officer. She snuggled up next to him, rested her head on his arm and placed her tiny hand in his. It was one of the saddest moments in his career. He felt a deep sorrow as he looked down on the little girl. But her eyes gazed upon him as if he were her biggest hero. He pondered how anyone could neglect this precious child.

CPS immediately removed the children from the home. The three-year-old threw a tantrum; screaming and crying out for her mother; who sat on a porch chair, almost emotionless. She smoked a cigarette, unresponsive to what was going on; almost in a comatose state. Throughout his career he carried the memory of that little girl to remind him of the precious ones that he swore to defend.

In Stephen's opinion, one of the most important aspects of the job is to observe your surroundings, even on those quiet afternoons, something he learned early in his career when he was an Explorer Scout. He was nearing the end of a shift when a call came in about a missing child. He remembered earlier that day while on a routine patrol he had seen a group of children playing in a yard near his beat and one of them resembled the missing boy.

Stephen: By being attentive, we were able to return to the home where the children were playing and find the missing child. He was returned to his mother. This was a satisfying experience which proved that being attentive pays.

When Stephen is off duty he can be found tending to his

farm in Texarkana. The farm has been in his family for almost 100 years; first bought in 1915 by his Great Grandfather.

Stephen: He raised chickens, cows and horses. He had several butcher shops in the Texarkana area until he died in the fifties. In the early 90's, my parents and I began a partnership with my aunt and uncles involving the farm. Several years later we bought them out. We have mostly registered Brahman cattle and a couple of Herefords cows. The farm is a place where I can unwind and regroup. It is part of me and a big part of my family history.

*If a teen stated that they wanted to follow in your chosen career path, what would be your advice for them?

Jeff: I would urge them to enter an explorer program in order to ride along with their local Police agencies to gain a better understanding of what is involved with being an officer. I would also encourage them to pursue a degree in criminal justice.

Stephen: I believe that if a teenager wanted to pursue a career in Law Enforcement, they should do all they can to live an unsullied lifestyle. They should focus on getting a sound education and doing their best to serve their community in which they live.

Welcome to the Brotherhood

Jeff Cottingham

Law Enforcement is an awesome institution that has been a very large part of my life for many years now. It has become at one time or another the supreme focus of all my energies. You pour your heart and soul into a career and what do you get? The simple answer is this.... you get a family. The brotherhood is not a family in the traditional sense. It is called the brotherhood, yet it is comprised of men and women willing to lay their lives down for you without hesitation. These men and women are willing to stand in front of you and protect you from evil when you may never have met before. There are no strangers in the brotherhood. There are simply family... members in particular that separately can be troubled and stumble but collectively are strong and brave. Courage and honor are the attributes of the family. We are not without our faults nor do we claim to be perfect. If we have never met let me tell you... My family and I will be here for you. In your darkest hours We will be there. In your times of need we will provide. In your times of anguish, we will comfort. It is more than our job requires... it is our pleasure to serve you. We ask only one thing in return. Late at night when the darkness comes, and you prepare to lay your head to rest... will you say a little prayer for my family. We will be out there protecting you until the daylight comes.

Police Officer Billy McCombs

With all of the risks involved with law enforcement there is the occasional call that just makes the police shake their head and chuckle! Those moments when the only thought they can muster is, "Seriously? Is this happening?" With as much disdain that Officer Billy McCombs has for drunk drivers; he had one of those "Seriously?" moments when he pulled over an intoxicated driver.

Billy was doing routine patrol when he got behind the drunk driver. He pulled him over for driving erratically and as he approached the truck; the driver hopped in the passenger seat and put a giant stuffed teddy bear in the driver's seat. He then tried to convince Billy that the bear was driving because he had been drinking and was not able to!

Officer McCombs started his career in law enforcement with the military police when he was 19 years old. There was no single person who influenced his decision to be a police officer. He simply always admired and respected the work of law enforcement.

Billy: You have to be born to do this job, I believe, to be good at it, because the pay is always substandard, and the thank yous come very few and far between.

He served with the Farmersburg, Indiana Police Department from 2000 – 2003. During that time, he served as the department's Chief of Police and K9 Handler. In fact, he and his K9 partner, a German Shepherd named "Gabe," were the only Officer/K9 duo in their county, as well as, surrounding communities. In 2003 he transferred to the Shelburn Police Department where he remains today as the department's Chief Deputy. In 2007 he also began serving with the Indiana Department of Defense Police.

It was the position of K9 handler that he enjoyed the most. The two did their part in the war against drugs by taking in several large quantity drug seizures. They were also the "Puppy Patrol" at the local schools; which is the equivalent of a DARE program. They taught children about the dangers of drugs and held demonstrations of drug searches.

For Billy, one of the most memorable calls the duo responded to was tracking an armed suspect, who was wanted for pulling a shotgun on a police officer. The trail led on for four miles; through waist deep snow and several creeks. They were able to track the suspect to a major state highway where he was picked up and given a ride to a local bar. With the help of Gabe, he was apprehended safely.

Among the positions that he worked in law enforcement, which include undercover drug busts, K9 handler, Chief of Police, tactical team member and patrolman today he can honestly say that he has "pretty much run the gamut of things you can do as a police officer."

In 2006 Gabe needed surgery for a twisted stomach and he passed away from complications stemming from the operation. Billy enjoyed working with Gabe, and the beloved German Shepherd will always hold a special place in his heart. Billy is now training a new K9 partner.

One aspect of police officers is their influence and reputation in the public. When Billy met a 16-year-old named Brady, he was working summers at IUPU I (Indiana University-Purdue University of Indianapolis) and the two became fast friends.

When Brady graduated from high school, he started taking basic college courses; though he was unsure which major was right for him. That was until the afternoon that Brady went on a ride along with Billy! Brady then changed his major to criminology and set out to become a police officer. He is now a police chief in a small department outside of Indianapolis and to this day; he credits Billy with why he chose a career in law enforcement.

Brady is just one of several people that Billy influenced to become a police officer. Billy has two brothers that served a short stint in law enforcement due to his influence, as well as, several friends that are currently officers.

Billy: I had many calls that have affected my life, both good and bad calls. I had to lock up a good friend that was like a son to me for armed robbery in another town, he confessed to me and I took him in. There are several calls that have affected me over the years involving children being hurt, and under aged drinking and driving fatalities that will haunt my soul until the day I die, but we don't talk of those. I believe I have become a bit suspicious of people as we all do, and sometimes might seem uncaring to people, but that is just part of the job. I still feel good when I help someone or catch a criminal and take them off the streets, so they can't harm anyone. I have been injured a few times in the line of duty, a few trips to the ER here and there, but nothing ever real serious. Thank God! I always strive to come home safely to my family.

One of the downfalls in law enforcement is that when they are off duty, they still carry with them everything that they see on the streets; it can be difficult to separate from. Billy feels that all of the negative that he has seen has caused him to become a strict parent (though his children disagree). He thanks his family every day for standing by him and appreciates the sacrifices they endured for him during his career in law enforcement. This includes his long hours away from home and all of the missed birthdays and holidays.

Billy: I could not do this job without their support. My 17 yr old son wants to follow in my footsteps and become a cop also, and I support him 100%.

*If a teen stated that they wanted to follow in your chosen career path, what would be your advice for them?

Billy: I would advise any teen that wants to become a police officer to make sure it is a career they really want to do, it isn't for everyone, and it is a thankless job, if you can handle that, then you might have been born to do this job. You have to do this job to help people, as well as helping yourself. It makes me feel good to help people, even if justice isn't always served, at least you can be there in someones time of need.

Police Officer James Williams

As Officer James Williams worked the undercover drug sting that hot April afternoon; he knew the risks and braved them in spite; he wanted to do what it takes to rid his corner of the world of drug dealers. Little did he know; life was about to change in every way possible for him. At this time, James worked for the Savannah County Police Department. On April 11, 2003 he and several other cops were working as undercover Narcotic's Officers, assisting with a drug buy. The suspect met with one of the officers in the hotel room to make the drug sale. As they followed each other outside one officer then attempted to arrest the suspect.

At this time there were three suspects, two of which remained in the car, with James standing near the driver's door. The third suspect was outside the vehicle. When the occupants of the car noticed he was being arrested, they decide to flee the scene but not before attempting to back over the arresting officer, as well as, their friend who was standing at the rear of the car.

When James saw that the lives of his fellow officer and the suspect were in danger. He instinctively dove into the window of the car and attempted to commandeer the vehicle. The two suspects in the car attacked James with a tire iron to eject him from the vehicle. When they knocked James out of the car they drove over his leg while escaping from the scene.

James had only seconds to decide what actions to take. Should he save the lives of others and risk his own or back off and let them escape, which puts the rest of the community in danger. He didn't have to think twice. He saw that a fellow officer and an arresting suspect were about to be run down, and he put his life on the line so that they can live. It was more important to James to save their lives than worry what could happen to himself in the aftermath. In spite of the injuries that he received, he has steadfastly claimed that he would not change a thing from that afternoon.

Since that day, James has had several surgeries to attempt to repair the damage in his leg and he returned to duty in January 2005. He was placed on light duty in the narcotics unit where he handled several different positions without needing assistance, like others thought he would need. Those include In-tell Officer, Evidence Room Officer and Front Lobby Officer at the Narcotic's Unit. He applied for several light duty positions advertised within the department and they refused him.

James' nightmares were just beginning. The pain from injuries received that afternoon pales in comparison to the pain of betrayal from his supervisors who were about to abandon him.

On March 1, 2005, a Sergeant in his department, notified James of an Inter-Office Memo asking for officers on a light duty status to apply for a position supervising community service workers.

However, after applying he was informed that he was denied the position for the fact that his previous injuries required him to wear a leg brace and that it would prevent him from safely operating a motor vehicle.

On April 8, 2005, James applied for another position, this time it was for a Customer Service Officer at the main Police Precinct. Once again, he was informed by two office employees, at the instructions of their acting Chief that he was denied the position due to the injuries he suffered on duty. He was being denied position after position because of the injuries to his leg but was also denied the right to a medical retirement.

On April 14, 2005, James then applied for the position of Tele-Service Officer at the Chatham County Annex Police Precinct taking walk-in police reports. Once again, the acting Chief had those same two officers from before to inform him that he was denied the position. This time, no reason was given. The names of the employees have been withheld to protect James from retaliation.

On July 15, 2005, the officer, who risked his life to save two people, was fired! He was handed his termination papers but was never been given a reason why. James later learned that a Major in the Savannah Chatham Metro Police Department, sent falsified paperwork to the State of Georgia's Peace Officer's Training Council claiming James had voluntarily quit his job without cause.

The Training Council issues certifications to police officers in the State of Georgia. Though, the council was never able to produce any paper work signed by James stating that he had quit, he was none the less, forced out of the police department.

During this time the City of Savannah Police Department and the Chatham County Police Department merged as one unit. The city and the county failed to agree on who was responsible to provide the assistance James was entitled to. Though the merger agreement clearly stated that "all employees were to be treated as equals no matter what their former department."

He now has a spinal cord stimulator in his back to help control the pain. With all of this, Chatham County refuses to grant James his medical retirement. Meanwhile, several officers have been allowed to be medically retired and one of those officers was injured while he was off duty. One of the officer's stated to the Savannah News Press that he was being medically retired because he could no longer wear a duty belt due to problems of a bad back.

During his law enforcement career James received several Letters of Commendations.

*March 9, 1995 ~ Finding and returning a purse containing credit cards and over $1900 to the owner who did not even know she had lost it.

*March 26, 1996 ~ Arrest of Three Individuals who escaped from another officer.

*December 5, 1996 ~ Saving the life of an individual who had attempted to hang himself, Officer Williams cut him down and performed CPR and revived him until EMS arrived.

*September 27, 2000 ~ Busted a group of teenagers who were stealing bikes from Walmart and repainting and reselling them

*November 27, 2000 ~ Received an award from MADD for large number of D.U.I. Arrests.

*May 2003 ~ Received an accommodation for placing his life in danger and preventing fellow agents from being injured on APRIL 11, 2003.

Since that afternoon in April, his doctor has since informed him that he would not be able to be employed as a police officer or accept any other type of employment that involves long walks, running or standing on his feet for long periods of time. He has been advised by his doctors not to lift more than 10 pounds and has been diagnosed with arthritis and RSD in his leg from the injuries he sustained on duty during the drug bust that went awry.

Each day people leave for work wondering what parking spot they will get; did they remember their cell phone or are they ready for that meeting. They usually don't wonder if some crazed drug dealer is going to try and take their life; a concern that many cops carry with them. Police officers have our backs every day. What happens when THEY FALL? Who has their back?

James' medical problems will affect him the rest of his life. His two favorite hobbies, fishing and fixing lawnmowers have become difficult tasks that often bring on pain.

He cannot carry his own grandchildren. He will not experience running through the yard with them, as they play and laugh together while kicking a ball or chasing lightning bugs. He was robbed of those opportunities by a drug dealer who did not want to go to jail! He did not see James as a human being. He simply saw him as an object; an obstacle in his way and he hit him with a tire iron and drove over him. James selflessly devoted over 12 years of his life to protect his community and honor the badge; only to be betrayed by the very government that he proudly represented. A government that also did not see him as a human being; just an object; an obstacle in their way.

NOTE: James is now starting college to embark on a new career. He would someday like to be a Special Education Mediator so that he can assist students and their parents to make sure they receive the proper education and that all avenues are open for them.

*If a teen stated that they wanted to follow in your chosen career path, what would be your advice for them?

James: I would tell them to think long and hard about it, then if they still wanted to pursue that career to find a department which offered medical retirement in case they got injured in the line of duty and to purchase extra disability insurance and to find a department that was in a union.

This article about Officer James Williams appeared in "The Spirit" newspaper.

"A Blue Hero/Savannah Undercover Agent Recognized for Outstanding Service"

BY Stephen Prudhomme
THE SPIRIT

As an undercover agent for the Chatham-Savannah Counter Narcotics Unit, James Williams wanted to keep his identity a secret. Yet his actions as a member of that unit thrust him into the limelight and ultimately earned him a number of honors as well as mention in an upcoming book about police heroes.

Along the way, he's endured a number of medical and job-related challenges. Williams, 47, is a resident of Pembroke. For the past 15 or so months, he's worked as civilian custodian in the evidence room at the counter narcotics office of the Savannah-Chatham Metropolitan Police Department. Williams walks with a cane and wears a permanent brace, the result of an incident that changed his life. On the afternoon of April 11, 2003, Williams says he and five other agents were making an undercover drug buy at the Days Inn on Mercy Blvd. Williams says two of the agents went to a motel room to make the "purchase" and escorted a man out to the parking lot.

As they stood behind the man's car, which was parked next to the motel, they struggled to bring the individual under control as they tried to arrest him. Williams, meanwhile, was standing next to the driver's side of the car and watching two passengers, one in the front passenger seat and the other in the rear seat.

According to Williams, the front seat passenger suddenly jumped into the driver's seat, grabbed the wheel and started backing up the car toward the two agents. Williams, with a gun in his hand, jumped into the car and struggled with the driver as he tried to prevent him from running over the two agents.

As the two men grappled and the car moved slowly backward, Williams says the rear passenger hit him in the right elbow with a tire iron, shattering the bone and forcing him to drop the gun. Williams says he continued to battle both men until he was knocked over the head with a tire iron and pushed out of the car. The car then ran over Williams' right leg, the same leg he had injured 18 months prior to that while seeking medical attention for the daughter of a DUI suspect.

The drug suspects fled the scene, but their freedom was short-lived; one suspect was captured within several days, while the other turned himself in a short time later, according to Williams.

The two men, along with the car, left their mark on Williams, who was transported to Memorial Hospital with tendon damage to his leg. Over the next five years, he had eight to nine surgeries and had to wear orthotics, along with using the aforementioned cane. "I have never been out of pain," Williams says.

Williams took several months off to recuperate from his injuries before returning to undercover narcotics work. "I primarily drove around and bought drugs," Williams recalls. In 2004, he went back for additional surgeries and missed four months of work, using up his vacation and leave time for income.

Unable to continue as an undercover agent because of his leg problems, Williams was assigned to a number of desk jobs in 2005. He did have a chance to go back on the streets, as a civilian community services officer, but turned down the offer. "I wasn't stupid enough to go out there and not be able to defend myself," says Williams, noting that he wouldn't have been able to carry a gun. "

I had met a lot of people through my work as an undercover agent, and I had no protection against someone who I might have arrested previously. They might want to get even with me."

When he didn't accept the position, Williams says he was fired for not being able to perform the essential functions of a police officer.

Although he collected unemployment, Williams did not qualify for any sort of benefits or disability. He blames that situation on the merger between the county and city police departments and his position as a county officer. "We were told city and county officers would be treated equally once the merger took place, but we weren't," Williams, a former County Officer says. "That was a bitter pill to swallow."

In March 2007, with his workman's comp about to run out, Williams says he was offered his old job back as civilian custodian of the evidence room. Williams credits that action to his frequent complaints to his superiors and other county officials. "The county did it because they knew it was wrong to fire me," Williams says.

Thanks to people like Jennifer Shaner, Williams' actions as a police officer are being recognized. Earlier this year, the Pembroke resident and a friend nominated Williams for a number of awards through the American Police Hall of Fame in Titusville, Fla. These include the Silver Star for Bravery, Purple Heart, Lifesaving Award, Outstanding Commendation and Honor Award for Public Service.

Kim Connolly, awards secretary for the American Police Hall of Fame, says it typically receives 150 to 200 nominations for various awards each year. A board reviews the nominations and checks the documentation to make sure it's in order but, according to Connolly, doesn't have the resources to judge a nominee's qualifications for the award(s). If the documentation is in order, Connolly adds, the board approves the nominations(s). The approval process takes an average of 30 days. Shaner says the awards are well-deserved. "He stepped outside to help someone else," she notes. "It was very brave of him to put himself in danger to help another officer. I believe he's a hero for what he did. This is our way of showing him he did a good job."

Charlotte Hopkins also wants to recognize Williams' bravery as a police officer, and she's including him in her upcoming book, "Heroes in Blue," profiling heroic police officers from around the country. Hopkins, who lives in Pennsylvania, says she was inspired to write the book because she doesn't like the treatment police officers receive from the public. "People don't see them for what they really do," Hopkins explains. "They risk their lives every day, get hurt protecting people every day." Hopkins says she read about Williams on his MySpace page and decided to include him in her book. "He's done a lot, even before the incident in 2003," Hopkins notes. "I wanted people to see him for what he is. He's done a lot of great things for the community."

Williams, who pursued a career in law enforcement because it offered benefits and a "lifestyle he could be proud of" along with a sense of helping out in the community, is attending college and wants to become an attorney. "I want to help police officers who find themselves in the predicament I'm in," Williams says.

Patrol Officer Linda K. Sims

Deputy Sheriff Pat Kelley

In the 1970's there was a rise in female police officers, some of that credit goes to Angie Dickinson and her role in the TV series, Police Woman. The show aired from 1974-1978 and Dickinson played the main character, Sergeant Suzanne "Pepper" Anderson. Patrol Officer Linda Sims was one of the ladies influenced by "Police Woman."

Linda was 28 years old when she chose law enforcement as her career. She was previously married to a cop where she learned firsthand knowledge, on the inside of a police officer's life. It was not until after they divorced that she decided to join the Police Academy herself.

She worked as a Reserve Officer for three years while she attended the Police Academy. Upon graduation she served the Blytheville Police Department as a Patrol Officer and Radio Dispatcher.

When Linda joined the ranks of police officers in the United States it was much to the dismay of many male officers. Men were still having a difficult time accepting women with a badge. Verbal harassment, the cold shoulder and a lack of respect were common place for women trying to break into this field. Not all men were this unacceptable but unfortunately; there were some.

Linda: We weren't respected by the male officers and had to work harder to prove ourselves. In the early 80's, women weren't welcomed into police work very well. We may not have had the physical strength as a male, but we had other strength that was needed to deal with female prisoners and even influence difficult male prisoners. Sometimes words are more powerful than muscles. I loved it and still wish I were working in it now. The saying is true, quote, "Once it gets in your blood, you can't get it out" end quote.

Women, like Linda, paved the way for females, like Deputy Sheriff Pat Kelley, to pursue law enforcement as a career. Both women answered cries of help, risked their lives for their community and felt the heartbreak of citizens struggling with broken lives and desperately needing a rope to cling onto.

Pat often answered calls that are intense and heart breaking; while others leave her standing there wondering why she was even called! For example, she had to respond to a complainant that was whining about children playing too loud at the park next door to his house. Who would actually find it wrong for children to be happy and loudly playing at a park? This is merely another example of how callous some people have become today. If someone is disturbed by the laughing and cheering of happy children at play, then living next door to a playground is not a wise decision.

A call that stands out to Pat came in on a hot humid summer day when she was called to do a wellness check on a family in town. This call was personal to Pat because she had known the family for some time.

When she arrived at the home of the double wide trailer, she noticed the door ajar. She knocked and hollered out that she was there and identified herself as a police officer. Though there was no response, she could hear a gurgling sound coming from a back room. She was overwhelmed with a horrible stench that she feared may be coming from a dead body.

The electricity had been disconnected and the temperature inside the home was as hot as she imagined hell would be like. She cautiously made her way down the hall towards the direction of the awful sound where she would discover they were the struggling cries of a baby boy. He was sitting in the middle of the bed in a pool of urine and feces.

He was so severely physically and mentally handicapped that he couldn't speak, walk nor eat with his mouth and had to be fed by an I.V. bag that distributed milk through a tube that was attached to a port in his abdominal area. The milk that was left in the bag had clambered and the liquid that was draining into the tube was rancid. He apparently had pneumonia or some type of major breathing disorder as he was in respiratory distress.

Pat: I stood there a second but for what seemed like an hour staring at this precious little boy that was left so alone totally helpless and dying. I was afraid to move him because of the tube but as I leaned over him after calling for medical assistance code 3, and went to comfort him, he looked up at me and smiled. He smiled, though he was fighting for his life with every ragged breath he seemingly stole from the grasp of Death himself, he smiled. EMS arrived quickly and rushed him to the nearest trauma center.

This serves as an example of how important it is for people to get involved, the police cannot be everywhere all the time and rely on citizens to help them find children who need them. The sick, injured, neglected and abused children are relying on adults to be their link to the police.

Pat: I don't know who placed that call that day, but they had to have been a messenger from God. Had I not been dispatched to that house, he wouldn't have made it through the night, so the doctor's said. That will forever stick with me. Though I lost so much time with my family due to the long hours I spent working, calls like that one makes me think that I chose the right career and made me thankful for the ability to help. God has blessed me in ways that I could never begin to explain. Though I've been through a lot of heart ache, through my faith in God, I've been able to maintain a positive attitude.

The baby and his siblings were immediately taken into Emergency Protective Custody. The mother was "subsequently charged with everything in the book" and lost all parental rights. The little boy has since been adopted by a wonderful family. He is now eating and walking and able to communicate. His siblings continue to visit him and though they live apart they have remained a family.

Pat was 25 years old when she decided to pursue the goal to become a police officer. She was working at a factory and hated it. She needed something different. She always enjoyed working with people and wanted to do something that would make a difference in their lives and in her community.

Her career began at the County Jail. Her husband and family were not supportive of her decision. They were convinced that she would never become a police officer and said she would be at the jail until she retired. Pat knew that they were wrong and let their chide remarks roll off her back.

In 1991, as a Jailer at the Lee County Sheriff's Office, she took on an excessive amount of overtime and performed numerous volunteer jobs. Being involved proved to be beneficial in the advancement of her career. Unfortunately, she lost valuable time with her family in the process.

The next phase in her career was with at Bishopville Police Department where she began as a dispatcher and Reserve Officer. She served with Bishopville for 13 years and during that time she worked as a field training officer, first line supervisor, undercover narcotics agent, criminal investigator and established the juvenile investigative unit.

As an officer, Linda learned that one of the toughest parts of the job for a cop is the unpredictability of it all. Linda had one of these moments during a routine patrol on a late-night shift. It was right at the crack of dawn and she spotted smoke in the distance.

As she approached the scene, she noticed a house flooded in smoke. She radioed for assistance, ran to the back door and called out to see if anyone would answer. When no one responded she entered the home.

Through the thick gray smoke, she could see someone lying on the couch, but he was not moving. She ran to his rescue, choking on the air that was filling her lungs with soot and carbon monoxide and though he was barely conscious she was able to wake him enough to get him safely out of the house. He was treated for smoke inhalation but thanks to his rescuer, Linda, that was the extent of his injuries.

Linda later learned that he was not sleeping, in fact, he was intoxicated and passed out. He was smoking a cigarette at the time and that caught the couch on fire. If it were not for Linda being in the right place at that exact minute, he would have suffered serious burns or even death.

When citizens observe the police on patrol they sometimes sarcastically respond with "don't they have anything better to do" or "they must be bored." If Linda would not have been doing one of those patrols, she would not have been there to save that man's life and that is why such patrols are so important. What could be better than saving a life on a routine patrol!

There were some lighthearted moments on the job for Linda. During their down time police officers can be relentless, just rousing each other. Linda learned this lesson early in her career. She just started her shift and the men were in a joking mood with each other when a call came in that put a quick end to that mood. The local funeral parlor called and reported that there was still life to a body that he was about to embalm.

Linda: I thought, oh my God, I wasn't real cool with the idea of going to a funeral home and feeling a pulse of a dead body to see if it was still alive.

Her Lieutenant informed her that the EMT's would meet her there, but she arrived before them. She was led to the body by the mortician. As she stood next to it, feeling for a pulse, in walked her Lieutenant and the EMT's. They were all laughing at the sight of her feeling for a pulse from the corpse. "They had set me up big time," she says jokingly. In spite of their jokes, Linda feels, "They were a group of fine fellas."

The most traumatic event of Pat's life, as well as her career, happened at Bishopville. She just left court after testifying on a DUI arrest that she made earlier that year and was heading back to work for a 12-hour night shift. She had her daughter with her and was taking her to her Grandmother's house before her shift started. There was a rain storm going on that made it difficult to drive. The grey skies blended with the wind and heavy rain drops making visibility difficult. The road beneath her became slick and the water competed against the rotation of her tires all making for a difficult and dangerous road condition. Though she drove cautiously through the rain, within minutes of leaving the courthouse they were involved in a head-on collision that took her daughter's life.

Pat: I spent weeks in the hospital then again at home in a hospital bed. My physical therapist was there five times a week and helped me regain motion in both arms. Once my upper torso had healed, I returned to work in late September in a wheel chair and worked desk duty daily until I was able to walk again in February, 4 months earlier than predicted! I went back on the road for a while before being transferred into investigations until the screws, steel plates and pins were removed from my right foot/ankle/leg the following July. After surgery, I returned to duty as a first line supervisor on the road until I resigned in January 2004.

After a long recovery she moved on to the Kershaw County Sheriff's Office in South Carolina and worked as a road deputy and investigator. She is now a school resource officer at a middle school of approximately 630 students. She works on the Gang Unit and Alcohol Enforcement Team.

Linda has since resigned her position at Blytheville due to health problems. She continues to stay in touch with the department and maintains contact through the officers. After all, you can take the cop out of the department, but you cannot take the department out of the cop!

*If a teen stated they wanted to follow in your chosen career path, what would be your advice for them?

Linda: Take the initiative to strive to do well in their education and stay away from the wrong influences. Building a strong character, is very important. Honesty and trustworthiness are a plus in helping other people to have confidence in your ability to help them. Up hold what is right and care for those who are less fortunate than you.

Pat: When kids say, "I want to be a cop when I grow up!" I've heard many officers tell them "NO! DON'T! Get a REAL job that pays you plenty of money, this job will break you and drive you crazy with the long hours and disrespect from the public." I tell them differently.

When one of the kids at my school expresses interest in law enforcement, I explain to them about the long hours, painful memories they'll rack up from the really bad calls, injuries they might sustain from fighting drunks and dopers, interrupted plans due to unexpected subpoenas to testify in court, negative feedback from the public/media, etc.

Then I tell them of the little boy whose mama loved crack cocaine more than her son and how God moved that concerned citizen to call 911 and the dispatcher who wasted no time in giving me the call to save a life. I support their decisions if they have the temperament for the job. Those who simply want to drive fast and rough people up and drag them off to jail, I discourage. We have enough of those out here all over the country. They're the ones the media has a field day with at the expense of those of us who actually give a rip about what we do and who we do it for.

In summary, if I had it all to do over, again would I? Yup. Sure would! Of course, I'd make some changes that would've allowed me to spend more time with the kids and of course I would've told Julie she had to stay home that day, but I'd still do it. No doubt about it. My son, Matt, who is now 20, has entertained thoughts of being a cop but has chosen to work for our local electric company instead. He's all I have left and I have to admit I am a bit relieved that he's not out here dealing with thugs and placing himself in the line of fire from these gangbangers out here, however, he's dangling 30 feet in the air from a harness playing with thousands of volts of electricity, hmmmm, ya think adrenaline addiction might just run in the family?!

A Policewoman's Prayer

Oh lord, I am a woman, not a man.
I am a Mother not a Dad.
I am a wife with responsibilities that men have never had.
I need understanding from all my peers,
that I am not here to take away a man's job.
I am doing it because I care.
I took the job to enforce the law,
to do my part in the fight to have justice FOR ALL.
To be professional, to make a career, Great Lord,
help me when they say I should not be here.
I work the long hours, face all the dangers,
and do the same things they do in law enforcement matters,
Grant me the respect like the others, for I am one.
Set aside for every other one,
Lord, being a policewoman is the most challenging job I
have ever done.
Be with me on my daily run, as you are with us all,
I thank you for the ability to enforce the law.

WOMEN IN LAW ENFORCEMENT HISTORY:

*Rose Fortune served as the first female police officer. She was a self-appointed sheriff of Annapolis Royal, Nova Scotia in the late 1700's.

*In 1910, Alice Stebbin Wells, petitioned the mayor of Los Angeles, Caifornia to hire her as the first female police officer in the United States. Her petition was granted and on September 12, 1910 she was hired by the Los Angeles Police Department. She was instrumental in organizing the International Policewomen's Association in 1915, as well as, the Women's Peace Officers Association of California in

1928, in which she served as their first president.

*Kate Warne was the first female private investigator in the United States. She initially applied for the position of secretary at the Pinkerton Detective Agency but was hired the next day as a private detective. It is believed that she and Allen Pinkerton were romantically involved. She was an excellent investigator and could change disguises and accents at the drop of a dime. It is Kate Warne who uncovered plans for President Abraham Lincoln to be assassinated on his train ride to the White House the day before he was to be sworn in as President. She also created the plans to smuggle the president into Washington under the guise of her "invalid brother." The night of the train ride she sat by the president's side all night. She did not sleep at all, leading them to utilize the slogan, "We never sleep." She remained armed and on guard. It is because of Warne that the assassination failed. She is one of the facets that helped Pinkerton Detective Agency become the success that they are today. She paved the way for women today who are now serving in the investigation and security field across the country.

Aubrey Steele is one of the women serving as a Security Officer today. She and her husband, Rob Steele own Portland Security and are just as strong and intelligent of a duo as Kate Warne and Allen Pinkerton. In 2009 Aubrey and Rob's Security Company received their first K9 officer; a black Labrador named "Raven."

Working together in law, Aubrey and Robb have learned to read each other's body language and judge the tone of each other's voice. Once on an evening shift, Aubrey heard Robb call in that he picked up an unstable person. His voice was "calm and monotone" and she felt something was wrong. As her blood turned cold and chills went up her arms, she knew that he needed help. She was three blocks away but rushed to assist him. When she arrived, the subject was swinging a large chain with a padlock on it and yelling "shoot me now!"

The security field has come far and because of Kate Warne, women, like Aubrey Steele, continue to thrive in that area.

Aubrey: We have come a long way, we have to have a spotless criminal history, we can arrest you, spray you, taze you, search you, mirandize you, and yes, even, shoot you, all within reason, just like a "real" cop. But, unlike "real" cops, we don't get the respect that is deserved.

Police Officer Ken Morris

Domestic violence calls can be the most dangerous situations for the police, particularly since they do not know until they arrive how bad of a situation they are walking into, all they know for certain is that the people are angry and not thinking clearly. Many are at the height of desperation and simply do not care what happens to them at that point. They feel they have reached the end of their rope and there is nowhere to go but down! Police Officer Ken Morris has answered numerous domestic violence calls and has never forgotten just how dangerous the situation can become.

Once while answering a "domestic," Ken arrived to see the husband holding his wife in a choke hold. He drew his gun and yelled for the husband to release her. The husband proceeded to pull her into the bedroom and back into the hall; all the while Ken's gun was pointed at him as he continued to demand that the wife be released.

Ken: He would not obey my commands until I started to curse him. Once I started cursing him then he paid attention to me. Some people do not care about a gun pointed at them, but they revert back to their upbringing when you curse them. Before that call I didn't curse people on calls. After that I learned that sometimes you have to cuss to get their attention.

The call could have ended with many different scenarios. Fortunately, this one ended safely. Ken and his partner rescued the wife and her husband was taken in unharmed.

The most extreme call he responded to was a murder scene investigation that appeared nothing short of a scene from a Hollywood movie. It was on January 3, 1996 when 65-year-old, Muriel Ausley, was found murdered and disemboweled on her bathroom floor.

Ken: Her organs were laying on the floor around her and some of her insides had been flushed down the toilet.

When Ausley's attacker was caught; Ken learned that he was a seriously disturbed man who had been previously convicted of raping a 76-year-old woman in her home. He also learned that Ausley was still alive when her killer began his torture and even derived a sick sexual pleasure from her murder.

Calls like this haunt the dreams of police officers. It's not so much what they were faced with but in knowing of the details of the pain that is afflicted upon the public. It will always be an enigma to them how people can be so twisted and cruel to innocent and defenseless people.

When Ken joined the City of Birmingham Police Department in 1983 as a Patrol Officer, he was not directly influenced by any one person, but he remembers always having good cops around him throughout his life. Several of his neighbors were cops. Ken's good friend had an uncle who was a cop and two of Ken's own uncles were police officers. The town he grew up in had several friendly officers. In some communities the police are quite stand-offish when it comes to forming a friendship with the public but that wasn't the case where Ken lived.

Early in his career at the Birmingham PD he learned that his aunt was once a police officer in that same department and he did not know that she was ever even a cop. He started there as a bike cop and is now a patrol officer. He is still getting used to being on "four wheels."

During his career, all of his injuries occurred by falling down hillsides. His first fall happened during a foot chase. Ken grabbed onto the suspect just as he was about to run down a steep hill. They both tumbled down the hill with Ken still holding onto him.

When they landed at the bottom the suspect was looking up at Ken and asking him if he was alright. There was blood streaming down the middle of Ken's face from landing head first onto a log and suffering a cut to the back of his head.

During a winter blast of heavy snow and ice he responded to a car accident that went over an embankment. Working at the scene, Ken fell over the hillside twice; landing on his back both times.

There have often been times when homeless people thanked Ken for arresting them while they were drunk or high. They claimed that his arrest saved their lives, but Ken stated that "they went and did their drug or drink of choice again anyway." It is always disheartening when that happens.

Teaching self-defense is important to him. Ken finds it rewarding to spread knowledge to as many as possible on how avoid becoming victims. He compiled a list of "30 ways" people can protect themselves every day. He obtained this information from numerous sources.

Ken: One great book is "Strong on Defense" by Sanford Strong, a retired San Diego Police Sgt. Another good book is called Be Alert, Be Aware, Have A Plan. Go to skiphall.com and look at the arm program. Skip is a mixed martial arts fighter. He has been teaching rape prevention for 19 years. He has taught classes for several high-profile companies. Also go to capisdowntown.com for more tips. Look up McGruff the crime dog for more tips. Another good book is "Gift of Fear" by Gavin De Becker. These are some tips for preventing a violent crime from happening to you.

You must decide now if you want to be a victim. Your safety is your responsibility. Knowledge is the key to preventing victimization.

1) *Be aware of what is going on around you at all times.*

2) *Be alert!*

3) *Have a plan of action.*

4) *Decide now what you will do if you are attacked - fight or flight?*

5) *If you fight, then fight to get away not to win the fight.*

6) *Your responsibility is to get away at all costs.*

7) *When walking down the street keep your head up with confidence and scan the area.*

8) *If you see someone suspicious look them in the eye long enough for them to know you saw them.*

9) *Scan the area before you leave or enter a building or car.*

10) *Park in a well-lighted area.*

11) *Avoid the bad areas of town.*

12) *Make sure your car is well maintained and full of fuel.*

13) *Have your keys out and ready when you're going to your car or to your home.*

14) *Change up your routine every day.*

15) *Keep a cell phone with you but don't walk around or drive around with it attached to your ear to where you are unaware of what is going on around you.*

16) *Do not trust anyone you do not know.*

17) *Keep your car and home doors locked.*

18) *Women - do not leave a bar with a man you do not know and trust and do not let your friends leave with a man you do not know and trust.*

19) *Do not accept a drink from a stranger without watching it being made by the bartender.*

20) *Watch what you wear and where you wear it, avoid wearing jewelry in bad areas of town or provocative clothing in bad areas of town.*

21) *If you are attacked do whatever you can to draw attention to yourself and the attacker. Scream, yell, honk the horn, yell "rape," "911" or "fire."*

22) *If you are carjacked and you are the driver, escape right away, wreck your car if you have to.*

23) *DO NOT GO ANYWHERE with the attacker. Each crime scene is more dangerous than the last.*

24) *Do not allow yourself to be isolated by the attacker and do not let him take you to an isolated area.*

25) *Stay calm and think clearly.*

26) *Dial 911 from a cell phone. The first words out of your mouth should be your location. You may be cut off and at least they will know your proximity.*

27) *Know more than one way to and from work and home.*

28) *Know the location of safe places like your local police department, fire stations and hospitals.*

29) *Wear loose fitting clothing when possible. You will never know when you have to run or fight.*

30) *Do not answer the door for someone you do not know.*

Ken: Remember that in any violent crime your chances of being injured are very high. If you realize this from the beginning, then you will be ready. Expect to be hurt no matter what. By expecting to be hurt your mind will take over and you will be surprised what your body can take. Ladies, you need to know that over 60% of rapes are committed by an acquaintance. You are more likely to be raped by someone you know than to be attacked by a stranger. With that said, you need to watch who you choose as friends. You never know what a rapist looks like. Do not drink alcohol on a date. Watch what you wear and where you go. Watch your actions. Too many men out there do not know what "no" means and too many women have said that "no means maybe."

This world is not perfect so do not run around naked or half naked and drunk and expect be treated like a lady. Respect yourself first and then you will be respected. Do not worry about any man that thinks you're a "Witch." Your safety is more important than any man's feelings.

*If a teen stated that they wanted to follow in your chosen career path, what would be your advice for them?

Ken: I tell all people who want to do this job to go to college and get a degree in something other than criminal justice. I want them to have a plan to fall back on in case this job isn't for them or they lose their job due to injury. I also suggest that they start taking lessons in ju jitsu or aikido. They need fighting skills to do this job. If they are not confident in their fighting skills they tend to get into more fights. If they are confident then they tend to talk their way out of more fights. It is funny how that works.

Lieutenant Brad Vanover

Deep in a late-night shift, Lieutenant Brad Vanover was on duty with only one other deputy; when a call came in about a domestic disturbance in progress in the town of Emory. Brad responded immediately and radioed to dispatch that he was in route to the scene. At that time, he learned that there was a gun involved. Brad felt his adrenaline rush and the defense techniques that he spent hours studying and preparing for kicked in to play. His sole concentration became that of rescuing and protecting the victim. This would be a defining moment in his career.

Brad: At this time scenarios started going through my head, I was breaking each one down trying to find the best course of action to take.

Dispatch then informed Brad that the victim had her cell phone on and continued contact with 911, which allowed them to over hear the subject threaten the victim saying, "he was going to send her to hell and anyone else that tried to stop him." He was repeatedly knocking her down and beating her with the pistol. Dispatch then informed the officers that the assailant and victim were leaving the scene. Brad and his deputy arrived moments after they left.

They found that the only people there were the victim's son and daughter-in-law, who had also just arrived at the scene. The officers made entry into the home with their guns drawn. They had to assure that the scene was clear and that the home was safe from the subject or anyone else who may have been involved. After they were assured that the area was secure, they left the home to search for the victim.

As Brad left the home, he again contacted dispatch to ask

if they had a last known location. He noticed an ambulance approaching the house and when attempting to make contact with the paramedics, dispatch radioed back and advised him that they had lost contact with the victim.

Moments later they learned that a man delivering newspapers in the area was carrying a police scanner with him and was able to get a description of the vehicle. He located the subject's vehicle and was, in fact, on the phone with 911 and following the subject down highway 515.

Brad was approximately 10 miles from the scene and without a moment to spare he radioed a Code 3 and was in pursuit of the vehicle's location. "Code 3" means, due to the emergency of the situation the officer is using his lights, sirens and excessive speed to reach his destination.

He maintained contact with dispatch and was receiving up to date locations of the vehicle. After 15 minutes, Brad was on highway 515 and fast approaching the vehicle. When he crossed the county line, he notified dispatch that he needed assistance from the Hopkins County Sheriff's Department. Meanwhile, he switched to "Code 1" (which means, no lights or sirens) but maintained his current speed.

Within two minutes he caught up with the complainant and was able to pull the vehicle over to the side of the road.

Brad: At that time, I positioned myself in the felony stop position. With gun drawn kneeling behind my patrol car door, I advised county that I had the subject stopped. When my back-up arrived on scene, we ordered the subject out at gun point and placed him under arrest. I went up to the victim and asked if she was all right. I advised the ambulance that the scene was clear and that they could move up to care for the patient. The patient was treated and transported. The subject was taken to the Rains County Jail and charged with aggravated assault with a deadly weapon and aggravated kidnapping.

Each morning when Brad pins on that badge he knows quite well that these calls can occur. Though he knows his safety and his life are on the line, he also knows that at any moment the safety and lives of the citizens can also be on the line. For this reason, his higher priority is for the people of his community to know that they are protected and in their times of need he will not hesitate to respond.

When Brad was promoted to Sergeant, he was given the responsibility of training new officers. During one of these sessions, he was showing a new recruit the different scenarios that they may encounter; when at that moment, a true-to-life call came in that would show the young officer the true dangers of the job. The officers received a call from dispatch concerning an unauthorized person on someone's property. As they headed back to their patrol car, dispatch advised them that weapons were involved. They glanced up at each other, acknowledging that things had just gone from bad to worse.

They jumped into their car and raced to the location. Upon arriving at the home, as they were about to pull into the driveway, the complainant came barreling around the corner holding a shotgun in the direction of the officers. Across the PA, Brad ordered him to drop his weapon only to be ignored. Brad ordered, twice more, for the man to drop his shotgun until he complied.

He and his partner rapidly pulled into the driveway and exited their vehicle, with guns drawn. Brad immediately checked the shotgun, upon verifying that it was in deed loaded, he emptied the weapon and secured it in the trunk of his patrol car.

When Brad questioned the complainant, he learned that someone made entry into his residence by crawling through the air conditioning vents in the ceiling. Brad told him to stay there while they checked his home.

First, they checked the perimeter and then made entry inside the home. They searched each room and were confident that no one was there. However, they did observe drug paraphernalia on the bedroom floor. When Brad questioned the man about it, his explanation was that the person who broke into his home must have planted it there.

Brad: At that time, I asked the complainant if he minded us searching the residence for more paraphernalia and other contraband, just in case they had left anything else. The complainant stated that he did not mind, and he signed a waiver for us to perform a search of the residence. Upon completion of the search we discovered more drug paraphernalia, a controlled substance that turned out to be meth and numerous other contraband items. The complainant was placed under arrest for possession of controlled substance and possession of drug paraphernalia.

Brad later learned that there never was a break-in at the man's home. In fact, the man was under the influence of meth and was hallucinating.

In the seven years that Brad has served in law enforcement he quickly rose through the ranks to Lieutenant. It all began for Brad when he was twelve years old. He and his father were driving down the road when, out of the blue, Brad looked up at his father and told him that when he grows up, he wants to be a police officer.

Brad: From then on, I knew that I wanted to do nothing else. I tried other jobs, but they never made me truly happy. After beginning my career in law enforcement, I finally knew what true happiness felt like.

While growing up, his role models have always been his mom, dad and uncle. His father always hoped he would follow in his footsteps, career wise. He worked as an electrician and Brad worked alongside him for some time, but it was never satisfying work for Brad. Though it was not something he enjoyed; he saw the happiness and satisfaction that the work brought to his father and that is what he hoped to experience. He wanted a taste of a job that was not just work but a gratifying career!

His uncle is a retired DPS trooper and is now a constable in Hopkins County. Brad remembered riding along with him as a teen. The exciting part for him was observing what happened behind the scenes. His uncle is the reason Brad is a police officer today.

Brad: My mom is the strongest woman that I know, she has overcome nearly impossible odds and has never had any regrets. She has been my anchor and my dad has been my chain. With them together I am the man I am today. I thank God every day that I can call them my parents.

He began his Law Enforcement career at the Lone Oak Police Department as a Reserve Officer. Only a year and one month with Lone Oak he was offered the position as full time Patrol Officer for the East Tawakoni Police Department. After less than eight months with East Tawakoni he was promoted to Sergeant and six months later was promoted once again to Lieutenant.

Even when the police are "off duty" they are always ready to assist a fellow officer. Brad and his peers have always held this dedication. Once when he and a few friends, also police officers, did get the night off they decided to load up their fishing gear and head out to the lake in East Tawakoni. It was approximately midnight when a call came across their police scanner for a fight in progress in the neighboring town of Emory. Yes, it is true that police officers carry a police radio everywhere with them, always wanting to be a stone's throw away from anyone that may need them...and on this night, it hit them even closer to home!

There were two female officers on duty to respond to the call. One was from Brad's department and the other from Rains County. She was also a good friend of Brad's and the girlfriend of one of the men who was there fishing with him. While in route the deputy struck two deer, which is equivalent to the force of hitting the side of a building. The next call was the deputy siting that she was in a 10-50 (wreck) and suffered injuries.

Brad: We were glued to that radio hanging on every word that came across. Just then the Deputy came across the radio, and just from the sound of her voice we knew that she was in trouble.

The men had heard enough! They left the lake; leaving behind their fishing gear and dashed to her aid. They were the first on the scene. The deputy was crying out from the extreme pain; proving that cops aren't machines but human like the rest of us. When her air bag deployed it caused injuries to her chest, head and face. One officer held c-spine, by placing both of his hands, one on each side of her head, to stabilize her spine to prevent further injury. All the while her boyfriend talked to her to soothe her fears and keep her calm. The remaining officers removed her from the vehicle.

Brad called for first responders and an ambulance. The fire station, where Brad also serves as a firefighter, informed him that there was a firefighter at the station on standby to assist.

Paramedics arrived informing Brad that the Flight for Life helicopter was in route to transport the deputy to a hospital in Tyler and requested additional units to set up a landing zone. At that time, the East Tawakoni officer had cleared the "fight in progress" call and had arrived at the accident scene to assist.

Brad contacted the firefighter to assist in setting up a landing zone for Flight for Life but was informed that he was the only one at the station. Brad and his fellow officer then drove to the fire station so that Brad can pick up one of the trucks. This way there would be two firetrucks and a police car to set up a clear landing zone for the helicopter. This is important because if there are any overhead dangers like power lines; they like them marked. After several days in the hospital, the officer made a full recovery and returned to duty.

*If a teen stated that they wanted to follow in your chosen career path, what would be your advice for them?

Brad: I would tell them to follow your heart. It takes a special kind of person to be in this line of work. You have to learn how to deal with the best and worst of people. You can't hesitate for a second if your life or a third parties' life is on the line, because a second might be all that you have. You will be faced with obstacles on a daily basis that will make you think, that will challenge you in every way possible. There might come a day that you stop and think twice about your profession in law enforcement. The people that last in this profession, are the ones' that truly love their profession. They also can't be all there, anyone that might have to kick down a door not knowing what might be on the other side waiting for them, or having to crawl into a carnage of twisted metal to sooth a crying passenger or driver of a vehicle that just wrecked, or to put yourself in between a man and his wife that have been fighting. A person that chooses this line of work as their profession is a special one. You won't be patted on the back or given praise all the time, you might not even get thanked after arresting an abusive husband. Just follow your heart, if this is truly what you want to do then your heart will tell you so.

FROM EUGENE AND NORENE VANOVER

On Brad's 12th year of life he informed me that he would like to be a police officer. I told him to do no drugs and no DWI's and I would support him. I am most proud of his profession and to move into the investigative side of law enforcement.

FROM BRAD VANOVER: A DEDICATION TO THE PEOPLE WHO ARE CLOSEST TO HIS HEART AND WHO HAVE INFLUENCED HIM THE MOST:

My sister Debbie, she's not only my sister but one of my closest friends.

I would like to thank Chief Neil Dent from Lone Oak PD, my first police chief. He took a chance on a rookie, fresh out of the academy and gave him his start at achieving his lifelong dreams and goal.

I would like to thank Chief Rick South from East Tawakoni

PD, my current police chief. He offered me my first paid position. I have learned a lot from this man and I am proud to call him my boss, as well as, my friend.

I would also like to acknowledge my extended family, the members of the East Tawakoni PD, East Tawakoni VFD, Point PD, Point VFD, Emory PD, Emory VFD, the Rains County SO, and Champion EMS. We might not always see eye to eye, but we always have each other's back. I am proud to work alongside each and every one of them.

Deputy James Heath

Every generation has a group of teens that are generally misunderstood by the public and the police. In the 70's there were the "hippies." In the 80's there were the "punk (rockers)." In the 90's there were the "skaters" and now in the millennium there are the "goths." Deputy James Heath is a pioneer among law enforcement to teach acceptance and understanding of the goth culture.

James: I am a cop who has an appreciation for gothic music and is more understanding of the goth culture than some people typically are. I make it a point to go out of my way to get to know all of the "Goth Kids."

When Deputy Heath was assigned to Speight Middle School, he found a small community of kids who were into heavier forms of Goth music, as well as, several kids leaning more towards Emo music. He understands the problems that goth students are going through and the obstacles they face to be accepted by their peers and the public. It helps them to know that there is an officer who does understand them. He knows the music they listen to. He understands and respects them and their culture. It is because of this that many students are more willing to talk to him.

James was given an opportunity once to address a group of Law Enforcement Officers about the Goth culture and hopefully was able to give them a better understanding of some of the youth that they may encounter when working. Many people mistakenly judge people that are different than themselves that they do not understand.

Myths of Goth teens include:

*Goths are a Satanic Cult - Some Goths are Satanists, and some are wiccan but there are also Goths who are Christian, Buddhist, Catholic, etc. There is no specific religious belief among Goths. Also, at the core of a cult is a leader and Goths do not follow a leader.

*Goths are Marilyn Manson Fans - Marilyn Manson's music is not even considered by some Gothic music fans to be Gothic. There is no hard and fast rule that says who is and who is not Goth. Some Goths are Manson fans, but Goths listen to a wide array of music. Gothic music can and does include everything from darker sounding classical music, to artists such as Bauhaus, The Cure, and Gary Numan.

*Goths are Evil - This myth was fueled when the media labeled the Columbine killers as Goths - They were actually fans of Marilyn Manson but of course a lot of people in the Gothic culture do not even listen to Manson or consider his music to be a representation of Gothic culture. In fact, most Goths are not violent.

*Goths hate everyone and want to kill people - Again this was fueled by the media after the Columbine shooting. Almost all Goths are against violence. Goths are generally kind and accepting of all people, regardless of their race, religion, sexuality and beliefs.

*Goths Always Wear Black - Wearing black does not make you goth and being goth doesn't mean you have to wear black. There is no dress code among the goth culture.

*Goths Are Depressed or Suicidal - People of all social

groups are prone to sadness or depression, so yes, like other cultures, some Goths are depressed, and some are not. Solely "being goth" does not make a person depressed. Most Goths will tell you that suicide is not a part of goth culture. Goths are intelligent and curious in nature allowing them to openly explore all emotions, including sadness.

*Goths Don't Fall in Love - Everyone falls in love at one point or another. To assume that Goths do not feel love is absurd. Goths enjoy being in love and some are romantic!
*Goths Are Gay or Bisexual - Goths very open minded and accepting of others, so people who are different in any way will generally feel more welcome from the gothic community. It has been my observation that Goths do not typically show prejudice towards other people.

When James was growing up, he always wanted to be a police officer, specifically, a North Carolina State Trooper. His family attended church in Goldsboro, North Carolina, along with many enlisted Air Force soldiers from the Seymore Johnson Air Force Base. It was there that he met, Howard Setzer, a Military Police Officer with the Air Force. They are commonly known as "Security Forces."

Setzer served as a mentor for James and other children at the church and often chaperoned their functions. He, as well as many of the other soldiers, often ate lunch with James' family after church on Sunday. Setzer later became a police officer with the Charlotte, North Carolina Police Department. He made the biggest impact in James' life and is the man he chooses to emulate today.

James also toyed with the idea of doing car stunts for movies and being a rock star. He first played drums as a hobby in his early teens. Shortly after, he turned 16 he went to work for the supermarket chain, Winn-Dixie. While there he cleaned floors, bagged groceries and stocked shelves. Upon graduating from high school, he entered the store's management training program and several years later he was managing his own store. He continued to play drums on the side and played in several bands. Some of the highlights of his music career include:

*Magenta's Turn - a noisy, post punk alternative band that played mostly at Christian Music festivals and Church Youth Group shows. They began around 1989. Magenta's Turn released the live album "Flowers" in 1994 on the Smear Records label. The live show that would become the album "Flowers" was also broadcast on television. They received a bit of radio airplay on North Carolina State University's radio station, WKNC. For several weeks, "Flowers" was the number one most requested song on WKNC's show, Resurrection Rock.

Another of their song's, "Shame," was extremely popular with the listeners of Rez Rock. The fans caused quite a frenzy when the band played the song "Flowers" live. It was quite a spectacle to see! James describes it as mosh pits with flowers flying through the air!

*The X-Ray Men - A branch off of Magenta's Turn that was similar in sound to their next band, Bunker! This band was basically "Bunker" with a name change and a new bass player.

*Bunker! - Another Magenta's Turn spin off, though a little more spacey than Magenta's Turn. Bunker! played secular shows with an ambient atmospheric sound with no vocals. The only real tie to Magenta's Turn was that it contained former members of Magenta's Turn.

*MindCircus (Gothic Metal) This was the last serious band he played in before giving up his attempt to make music his career. It was when this band broke up in 2000 that James was prompted to pursue his career in Law Enforcement.

Through the years, James has made recordings for his good friend J. Lindsay Wright, a sound engineer from Atlanta, Georgia. James and Lindsay were in a band together (in Raleigh NC) many years ago that never really went anywhere. Over the years Lindsay asks James to play on certain recording projects and that is something that continues on even today.

It was while he was managing at Winn Dixie that he made friends with officers from the Durham North Carolina Police Department. Once again it ignited his thoughts in a career in law enforcement. He still was not quite ready to make that move. He chose to work at an electroplating shop. He had a limited schedule, and this gave him time to contemplate what he wanted to do next.

When word spread that he left Winn-Dixie; an old band mate from Magenta's Turn contacted him and asked him about resurrecting the band. The band originally performed in the Christian rock scene; often at church youth group functions and Christian music festivals. They planned to continue playing some Christian rock but also played in clubs and bars. That enabled them to have more gigs and play on a more regular schedule than previously. James continued to work at the plating shop while playing drums on the side. The whole while he knew that it was a career in law enforcement that he wanted.

Magenta's Turn was more than just a Christian rock band they were a group of young men with the compassion and integrity that the teens needed to see at that time in their lives. Often after their concerts the band would mingle with the teenagers and would sit and talk to them. This was the first opportunity that James had to mentor teens.

He and his band mates talked to the teens about life, their friends, their goals and sometimes their problems. Never missing a beat, the band always listened to what the teens had to say. There were a few who decided, to accept Jesus Christ in their life.

One of the band's crowning moments was when they met a runaway from Florida. She had been missing for several months. After she listened to their music and talked to the band about the problems, she felt she had with her parents she made the decision to return home. The band called her father who was ecstatic at the news and was more than willing to come and get her!

In the fall of 2000, at the age of 35, James knew that it was time to pursue his law enforcement goal. Police officers are born with the innate desire to protect and serve; they also seem to know when the time is right to take that leap! It is something inside of them that tells them, that is where they need to be, and this is what James felt.

James: I put in applications at 2 agencies just to see if a guy my age with no previous law enforcement work history could even get an interview. I figured at least I might be able to learn what I needed to do to prepare myself. I started talking to LEO's (law enforcement officers) when I would see them and tried to find out more about what I should do to get into this line of work.

The first call he received was from Wilson County Sheriff's Office. Shortly after, he was offered an interview with Wake County Sheriff's Office but respectfully declined. In 2001, he accepted a position with Wilson as a Detention Officer (Jailer). Once there, he attended a Detention Officer Certification School. He was a jailer for five years and worked through the ranks to the Lieutenant's position.

He went back for further education and took the Basic Law Enforcement Training. He was older than the other cadets and most instructors. Some may feel intimidated by this; James just wanted to learn all he can, not swayed at all by the age difference.

In 2006, at the age of 40, he graduated from Basic Law Enforcement Training and was appointed the position of Deputy Sheriff. He continued his work at the jail, and eventually had opportunities to participate in the field training for detective, civil process, and criminal patrol.

He was excited to gain the vast experience and education from the many branches of law enforcement. He was then transferred to the SRO Division. There he attended School Resource Officer Training and maintains the position of School Resource Officer today.

James: One popular question from the kids is whether or not

*I have been shot and whether or not I have shot someone.
They seem disappointed that the answer to both is "no."*

There is a difference between "Deputy Sheriff" and
"Police Officer." A Sheriff is elected to their position so they
"hold office" for as long as the voters continue to elect them.
A Deputy is appointed to his position by the Sheriff. A Police
Officer is hired by the city and answers to a Police Chief who
is hired not elected. The Sheriff is the highest-ranking Law
Enforcement Officer in a County. This is why many Sheriffs
refer to their agency as an "Office" rather than as a
"Department."

James is on the Advisory Council for the Mediation
Center of Eastern Carolina which sponsors several
programs one of which is "Teen Court" which helps troubled
youth who have been charged with a crime get the help they
need to change their behavior and further helps them keep
their criminal record clear. James participates in a variety of
activities sponsored by the Wilson County Law Enforcement
Officers Association.

The group, WCLEOA, consists of police officers, state
troopers, deputy sheriffs, detention officers and probation
and parole officers throughout Wilson County, North
Carolina. James has recently joined the membership ranks
of the WCLEOA. Each Christmas he volunteers with their
"Shop with a Cop Program." On these outings they all meet
at Walmart on a Saturday morning; where they are assigned
a child and given money to spend. They then enjoy a day of
Christmas shopping! The group, WCLEOA, once held a fund
raiser for a police officer who was shot in the line duty and
another fund raiser to build a handicapped accessible
playground.

For James, working with teens is his most gratifying work.
The teens have grown to know the officer well and trust him.
For some teenagers, he is the only officer they will talk to in
times of need.

*James: I get visited at my office many times by parents who
"just want to meet" the cop that their kids talk about*

constantly. This makes me feel good since one of the roles · of an SRO is to be a positive role model and someone in law enforcement that kids feel comfortable talking to. That is a big thing right there. Being someone, the kids will talk to. It is important that the kids feel that you are accessible and that they can trust you.

While most of us will never know if what we do makes a difference in someone's life. It is guaranteed that what James does makes an impact. You can't work with teens and "not" make a difference. Each opportunity he gets to work with the students changes who they are and the type of adult they will grow to be. Whether it's a kind word, a pat on the back or a shoulder to cry on, he is always there for them and they know it. Sometimes all they need is to know someone is there for them.

Teens need someone who won't judge them, who are looking out for their safety and who truly care! Many teens today, don't have that in their life. For example, each time he sits down and just listens to one of the female students tell him about what a bad week she had and how hard things appear to her; James has an opportunity to make a difference. An opportunity to mentor, an opportunity to give that young lady the answers and guidance she needs to make the right decisions.

These are life impacting moments that are offered to James every day. Each time he sees a young man about to make the wrong decisions with drugs or gangs, he has the opportunity to help stop that. He may not always be successful at that moment, but he is always successful in changing that person in a better way and giving them the life skills, they will need and use.

The next time you enter a high school and see a police officer monitoring the halls, remember, this could be an officer who just may be making the differences in our teenagers' lives as Deputy Heath does at Speight Middle School. Perhaps fifteen years from now, somewhere in North Carolina, there just may be a police officer who sits down with someone who asks them, "what made you want to be a cop" and his answer will start with, "when I was in school, I met Deputy James Heath."

*If a teen stated that they wanted to follow your chosen career path, what would be your advice for them?

James: First thing I would recommend is to try to get into a program like Law Enforcement Explorers and too try to do some ride along time with a law enforcement agency. This might help you decide if you really want to do this.
The next thing I would do is find out what the requirements for certification are in the state you intend to work in. Find out the minimum age for going to basic school and for being hired as a Law Enforcement Officer. For example, you can be hired by a Police Department at age 20 in North Carolina, but you must be 21 to be hired by a Sheriff's Office. You can go to school at 19 if you will be 20 when you graduate. When you have that kind of information you can start to make plans to make this a reality.

If you are planning to be a Law Enforcement Officer go ahead and start thinking and acting like one. By this I mean to follow the law and keep your record clean. You will not be able to be certified if you have certain things on your record. This will vary from state to state but most states do have some sort of background check before you can even go to basic school. Also, you need to know that you may have to take a mental/psychiatric evaluation and you may have to take a polygraph test. Now is time to prepare for your polygraph by making sure that you do the right things. Think about what you do and who you hang around with now, if you plan to be a Law Enforcement Officer in the future.

FROM JEREMY OVERMAN; A STUDENT AT SPEIGHT MIDDLE SCHOOL:

"I met Deputy Heath during lunch at Speight Middle School a few weeks ago. Well, he rather met me when he recognized the picture of the band 'Moonspell' on my shirt. Everything started out sharing experiences as musicians, though soon evolved into something much more. It seems he actually understands me for who I am (as a goth through my own train of thoughts) and, unlike most common stereotypes, he likes me for who I am. Ever since I met him (and even unintentionally before I met him) he has given me and my family great advice as well as he became a great friend. I have never met anyone like Deputy Heath, either as an officer of law, or as a great friend. I don't know what I would do without him."

Chief of Police Serena Booth

As a true "hometown girl" Police Chief Serena Booth attended a small high school, small colleges, is a member of a small church and now works at a small police department. It's the closeness that is brought out in small communities that she has always been fond of in all aspects of her life.

She always knew in her heart that she wanted to be a cop; though as a teenager, she did not receive the same encouragement from most teachers. Her friends and classmates thought it was pretty funny - Serena was pretty laid back and LOVED to have fun. Because of her slightly wild personality, the thought of her being a police officer was indeed a bit comical.

On the first day in her Business Management class in high school the teacher passed out forms asking each student to write down their contact information and the type of business they would like to own someday. She wrote down her address and telephone number and promptly returned it to the teacher. He glanced at her slip of paper and immediately called her back to his desk.

She knew what this was about; she did not complete her form. When she approached the desk, he looked up at her and said, "You did not put down a business here, Miss Whitney." She responded, "I know...I want to be a cop." The teacher smirked, and the class laughed! Serena laughed at her own comment. However, she went on to complete his course; earning recognition for achieving a 99%. The business she did choose was a surf shop.

In January 1990, her grandfather, whom she affectionately refers to as "papaw," offered to pay her way through college if she moved to Odessa, where he lived. With hope and excitement, she packed the next day and set out for west Texas to achieve her dream. She missed the deadline to start the winter semester at the law enforcement academy, so she took a few college courses and waited for the spring semester.

While attending the academy she worked in undercover narcotics as an informant. On November 21st (just 11 days after her 21st birthday) she graduated from the Odessa College Law Enforcement Academy. Upon graduation she took the TCLEOSE exam (Texas Commission on Law Enforcement Standards and Education). She went on to work as a Reserve Criminal Investigator for the District Attorney's Office. Serena describes it as a fancy term that basically meant for her "Narcotics Investigator."

While working undercover on one particular assignment, she was meeting with a C.I. (confidential informant) at the C.I.'s home when the drug dealer showed up there. Serena was confusingly swept into a closet by the C.I. to hide until the dealer left. The dealer was screaming threatening remarks in regard to "an undercover narc." He knew the narc was a female, as well as her age and that she had blond hair.

Serena: I heard rummaging through the house, but for some reason he didn't get to the closet I was in. (I believe in God's divine intervention, not "luck" or "chances" and that was why he never found that particular closet door) I had on a body mic but couldn't say anything of course! It was frustrating. I also remember being in there frantically looking for a wig or SOMETHING to cover my blond hair!!

When the dealer left, Serena signaled to the officers outside that he had gone. He was several blocks down the road when officers pulled his car over. They found a small handgun in the front seat.

Serena: It's VERY difficult because you never know who you're dealing with or if they've already sized you up as soon as they've laid eyes on you.

During her rocky career she felt the sting of betrayal from some law enforcement agencies. She continues to have encounters with peers who believe that "a woman's place is at home, in the kitchen, barefoot and pregnant."

She has managed to escape serious injuries, though minor injuries are par for the course. She twisted her back due to resistance during some arrests. Someday the public will learn that if you resist arrest, you will only go to jail tired.

Serena learned that on most calls where the complainant is elderly and alone, they just need someone to talk to. The elderly have so much to offer and teach, yet society tosses them aside. Some people wonder how God allows so much loneliness in the world. It's not that he allows loneliness, after all, he gave us each other. There are too many people in the world for anyone to ever be lonely. God didn't disappoint them - we, as a society, have disappointed them.

Among the perks of being a police officer there was one more surprise in store for her! That was when she met Lynn, the man who would become her husband. They worked in sister cities, Lacy Lakeview and Bellmead and were always there for each other as back-ups on calls and traffic stops. In 1997 they attended Police Emergency Driving School together where they first started to bond. She says that, evidently, it was love at first sight.

Serena: I flippantly told 'that Booth guy', "If you're ever in the area, hollar..." You know like officers always say to each other. Well, he did. I was tuning my radar when I looked up & saw him walk outside toward my patrol car. I forgot what I was doing! He was so cute. We're more in love now than we were then. We've been through so much & people can plainly see that we're stronger because of it. Women always ask me if he has a twin, or a brother or if I'd clone him."

They only dated for a few days when Lynn opened his heart and proposed. He affectionately told her that she reminded him so much of his late mother, Patty, who died from cancer at age 38, in 1990. Lynn is her biggest influence - motivating her to become a better police officer and a better person.

Serena recalls once when she responded to a domestic disturbance call that involved a weapon. She was the only officer on duty and Lynn knew this.

A fellow officer in an adjoining city also responded but that didn't stop Lynn from worrying that Serena was in eminent danger. He drove as fast as his squad car would take him to have Serena's back once more.

Serena's children are at the center of her world. There are her 2 daughters (Alli, 18 and Aimee, 10) and her step-son, Adrian (17). He has been alienated from the family, but Lynn & Serena remain prayerful.

Serena: We don't know why some things happen, how people can be so evil, but we know there's a mightier work behind the scenes. And, He knows every detail. That's all that matters. The girls are terrific and bless my life and heart so much. I never would've thought dancing around the living room with my children would be so much fun. They ALL fill my heart - near or far. Nearly losing both girls (Alli as an infant and Aimee during childbirth) helped me to realize how precious they are. I could never take them for granted and will never understand parents who do so.

It is difficult for Serena and Lynn when their careers clash with their marriage. Her scariest moment occurred the day before their eighth wedding anniversary when her husband was involved in a shootout. Needless to say, their anniversary dinner was filled with silence. Serena seemed to be in a daze for a couple of days following at the reality of knowing "what could have been."

Because of someone who did not want to go to jail and

only looked upon Lynn as a target and not a father and husband, she could have spent her anniversary as a widow. It was a numbing thought.

The crime-fighting duo take pride in seeing the police and the public unite. So, it is important for them to stay active in the community off duty as well. They are active members in church and hold their church family close to their hearts.

Serena: We base our marriage, our lives, small decisions, big decisions, and decisions regarding parenting our children on God.

They are a family of horse lovers, who's best family moments are spent boating and traveling. Lynn and Serena find a peace taking long rides on the motorcycle Serena got Lynn for his birthday. They also enjoy the festivities of Pow Wows. Their family trees branch into a combination of native heritages - Lynn (Comanche) and Serena (Kickapoo/Apache and Comanche). She teasingly throws in Scottish/Irish as an explanation for her fairer, although not too fair, skin. Their heritage is important and meaningful to them.

Serena also does freelance photography, models and acts. "They're simply occasional hobbies - just something to do that's totally off of law enforcement! Except for photography, I guess!" Hobbies are important for police officers. It gives them a chance to step out of the world of crime, abuse and assault and into a breathtaking world of happiness...if only for a few hours. A chance to reconnect with the realities of knowing that there are still peaceful and beautiful parts of the world.

Serena has done plenty of print modeling, commercials, theater, and in November of 2008 at 39 years young, she competed in her first beauty pageant in the Miss/Mrs division, with 18 other contestants ages ranging from 19 to 52, she walked away as 1st Runner Up and Swimsuit Winner. "I thought I was going to fall over, laughing! It was a great experience & one of those things I can add to my 'at least I gave it a shot' list! I'm a firm believer in doing all that you can, jump in with both feet - live life. I don't want to be sitting in a rocking chair one day, looking back on my life and say, 'Why didn't I try...?'"

Lynn, Serena, and the girls were honored in a traditional naming ceremony performed by Pastor Jack Neima (Lakota) of Buffalo River Indian Baptist Church in Waco, Texas on Mother's Day. Pastor Neima, Arby Littlesoldier (Lakota) and Barry "Kicking Bear" Byers are Serena's mentors and those she holds closest to her heart. Littlesoldier is, in fact, the great-great grandson of Sitting Bull.

Serena has come a long way from when she began her career with Ector County Sheriff's Office in Odessa, Texas. The morning of May 14, 2010, she was appointed Chief of Police for the Lone Oak Police Department and that very evening she walked across the stage as a graduate of Paris Junior College.

In 2005 she made the Phi Theta Kappa National Honor Society, National Dean's List in 2006, was granted her Special Investigator License in 2008 and earned her Master Peace Officer License in 2009. Serena later resigned from Lone Oak and in October 2011, she was appointed Chief of Police in Point, Texas.

*If a teen stated that they wanted to follow in your chosen career path, what would be your advice for them?

Serena: Unfortunately, we women still hit major obstacles in this field. Not only trying to "prove ourselves" but dealing with occasional insecurities or jealousies of fellow officers and/or their wives. This isn't the norm, but it has been a problem. It's been trying, to say the least. Sometimes my efforts to put their minds at ease works; sometimes it doesn't. But there's nothing I can do about it & I've certainly not lost any sleep over it.

I wish some of these guys would consider for a second how they would feel if their daughter, mother, wife was being treated unfairly or singled out. It can get to you - I don't care who you are, especially when you're just starting out - what a "welcome to law enforcement"!

*There've been a few officers who made a positive impact -
Jerry Davis (Ector County), Donny Harland, (TSTC), Mike
Nicoletti (LLPD), Rob Williams (TSTC & ADTF), Neil Dent
(LOPD), Randy Kirkpatrick and Charles Dickerson (RCSO).
They either said something or did something that
encouraged me and/or boosted my confidence.
Unfortunately, you don't really forget the ones who tried to
beat you down, but you hold dear to your heart the ones who
picked you right back up & said, "Go get 'em, kid."*

Sergeant Rodney Thompson

July 25, 1998 started off as any other day for Sergeant
Rodney Thompson, but it would end as anything less than
ordinary and leave Rodney fighting for his life. He was
originally scheduled to be off that day but switched shifts
with a fellow officer so that he can attend a volleyball
tournament in the following week. While working the second
shift (3:00 – 11:30 pm), he was typing a report at the
department office in Rustburg, Virginia when a call came
through dispatch of a suspicious male with a gun.

The suspect was attempting to have stereo equipment
installed in his vehicle, but his credit card was declined. He
told the store clerk that he would be back with the money.
The clerk noticed when he went to his car that he pulled a
gun and left the store. His aggressive tone and manner
made the clerk fear that he was about to commit a robbery.
Sergeant John Reiger and Deputy Leo Owen were nearby
and responded to the call. Rodney contemplated whether to
respond or to stay and finish the report; hesitating before
making the decision to respond.

When Officers Reiger and Owen arrived at the store they
notified dispatch and informed them that Hawkins had left
the scene. Rodney was near the Campbell County and
Lynchburg City lines when he learned that Hawkins had
crossed over into Lynchburg, outside his jurisdiction.

Rodney's sergeant granted his request to enter Lynchburg to search for Hawkins.

In minutes, Rodney noticed a white male matching his description (blue jean shorts and white t-shirt) and radioed to dispatch that Hawkins was located. He also requested a back-up unit at his location. He recalls that it was 4:16 PM.

When he pulled his car over, Hawkins looked over his shoulder at him, turned back around and continued walking away from the officer. Rodney noticed he was doing hand gestures with his shirt and suspected that was where he hid the weapon. He exited the vehicle, with his gun drawn (due to the fear that he was armed) and ordered Hawkins to stop and turn around.

Rodney ordered him to raise his hands and lift his shirt (a search for weapons). As soon as Hawkins arms went in the air Rodney noticed the handle of a gun. He ordered Hawkins not to move as he approached him (gun still drawn). Upon retrieving his weapon, Rodney escorted Hawkins to the front of his patrol car. In the process, Rodney noticed a knife with a clip in Hawkins front pocket. After placing Hawkins on the hood of his car he disassembled the retrieved gun (a necessary and important step).

All the while, Hawkins was continuously rising from the hood of the squad car and insisting that Rodney was harassing him and following him and that he had done nothing wrong. Rodney then pulled out his mace and ordered Hawkins to take the knife from his pocket and place it on the car or toss it on the ground. Hawkins only responded with, "what knife."

Rodney: Hawkins then removed the knife from his pocket (still closed), cuffed it in his hand while covering his face. At that time, Hawkins was ordered one final time to throw the knife on the ground or he would be sprayed. Hawkins commented, "don't spray me, that shit will burn." At that time, you could see the "fight or flight" in his eyes and as I unleashed a stream of mace, Hawkins took off running.

Dispatch was notified with Rodney yelling, "Campbell, I

am in foot pursuit!" The chase lasted ¼ mile. It went through a parking lot, across a culvert, through a yard and garden and into the back lot of a garage. During the chase, Hawkins lost his shoes and Rodney was able to catch up to him. He sprayed Hawkins with mace once more, spraying himself at the same time. When Rodney caught Hawkins he attempted to take him to the ground and a fight pursued between them.

Due to the mace stinging his eyes, everything was a blur to Rodney and he assumed that Hawkins was throwing punches at him, so he was throwing punches back. At this moment, it is difficult for Rodney to remember what all happened. He recalls that he was backing up, yelling, "if you move mother fucker, I will blow your god damn head off."

Hawkins lay face down on the ground wiping his face. Rodney continued to back up until he noticed where his can of mace landed when it was thrown. He then realized he stepped on something; looked towards the ground and saw Hawkins knife lying there. It was covered in blood. Rodney describes the scene as a triangle with Hawkins on ground, mace can on ground and me standing on knife – all 20 feet triangular from each other.

The temperature that day was about 90+ degrees. He quickly started to feel extremely hot, so he pulled his bullet-proof vest away to get air and blood began to instantly flow from his armpit and sleeve area. As the blood crept down his chest towards his waist, he felt it gushing out from the bottom of his pant legs. There was so much blood that seemed to be pouring out so fast that Rodney didn't know where he was bleeding from.

Rodney: I called dispatch and advised "441-Campbell.... Campbell, I need backup and I need rescue – I think I have been stabbed." Campbell to 405 (Sgt. Reiger) is 441 advising that he has been stabbed.... (me interrupting) "YES! Campbell, I need rescue" The time was 4:22 PM. Everything happened in 6 minutes.

When Sgt Reiger arrived, he pulled up behind Rodney, who was still holding Hawkins at gunpoint. Weak and unable to withstand anymore, Rodney collapsed on the hood of Sgt. Reiger's squad car and he dropped his gun on the ground. Reiger handcuffed Hawkins and secured him next to his vehicle. He immediately started first aid on Rodney.

Rescue soon arrived to transport Rodney who had never lost consciousness. He was filled with fear because of the blood that was still spurting out of him. Thoughts about his family were racing through his mind. Where were they? Was he going to live to see them again? His family was actually 20 miles away and were about to receive the news that Rodney has suffered life threatening stab wounds. They were told that his chances of surviving surgery were slim and that they should contact a preacher.

The surgeons worked for eight hours to repair the damage. They had to break open his rib cage to perform an open-heart surgery, which included a sternotomy, a clavicular, a thoracotomy. During his surgery he coded twice and was successfully resuscitated back.

The knife entered him twice. The first stab entered his trap muscle, the largest, most tense (and sometimes painful) muscles in the shoulder. The second stab from the knife was just under his clavicle bone. It pierced his heart severing the subclavian artery and subclavian vein completely in two. A hematoma formed on his lung from severe blood loss. Doctors later determined that Rodney lost 70% of his blood at the scene of the fight. His youth and top physical condition helped him to survive.

Following surgery, he was in excruciating pain and had 50 staples in his chest. He was transferred to the Surgical Intensive Care Unit where he remained for several days. Within the week his pain was still so extreme that he was not able to sleep. The doctor ordered the nurses to "pump him full of morphine until he passed out" and prescribed two Restoril to sleep better. The combination of the pills and the morphine caused Rodney to go into cardiac arrest. But no one was aware that it was happening because earlier that night the nurses removed his catheter and forgot to place the heart monitor back on his finger. A nurse happened to walk past his room and saw him in convulsions. He had coded again! Procedures were started immediately to revive him and get the medications out of him immediately. His family was once again called in to face the inevitable.

While Rodney lay in his hospital bed fighting for his life, his family stayed by his side, praying for any sign that Rodney would survive his ordeal. With every twitch of the eyelash, with every breath that he took they watched in cold silence hoping that he would would open his eyes. They stood nervously by listening to each beep from the heart monitor, knowing that his body was fighting to stay alive and hoping against hope that that he would not go into another cardiac arrest.

His sister, Angie, was about to break. Standing idly by was not her strong point. She sat down to write out the thoughts that were racing through her mind. She used the pen and paper to speak the words that she wanted so much for Rodney to hear. That night in the hospital, Angie wrote him a letter.

Tuesday, 4:45 AM

Mom and I came up to the hospital after the nurse called us saying that you had stopped breathing and had been emergently reversed. How terrified we were driving here, not knowing what to expect. You have had such a rough time – your pain, incision, chest tubes, nausea with eating. Now you are finally sleeping, breathing okay despite on 100% face mask. Your heartrate is down to 104. You're awakening with an extremely wild look in your eyes, looking straight ahead with your eyelids weighing 100 lbs. each (looking that way).

I don't know whether you know that we are here, will even remember us at your bedside...but I hope you felt and will continue to feel that undying love that we have for you. I never cried so much in my life as I did Saturday night as I heard mom say that you were hurt an in critical condition. The thought of losing my one and only brother would have killed me too.

You are so dear to so many as we have all seen over

these past couple of days. You are most dear to us. Please rest and take care of yourself. This will be a long recovery, both mentally and physically. I have no doubts that you are the one person who could face such circumstances and overcome all with your strength, courage, and faith – To my hero!

I love you,

Angie

The following morning, he awoke around 6 AM to find his family at his bedside. He was still wearing his oxygen mask which he quickly ripped off and asked them why they were there. They responded, "you don't remember what happened last night?" Fortunately, he did not remember!

Rodney: As the days passed, I started remembering everything in slow motion, it appearing that they were hitting me and the "bright light" in the background and everyone appearing as if cartoon people. Then I remembered nothing else. The only explanation that they could give him was the "hitting" was the doctors trying to keep me awake and I wanted to close my eyes and go to sleep. I was released seven days later to go home for a long road of recovery.

During his recovery he stayed with his parents who cared for him through many days of pain, suffering, rehabilitation, medications and depression. They never left his side. Their strength and encouragement is what he needed to survive from one day to the next. They never let him down. To the world Rodney was a hero but to Rodney it was his parents and his sister, Angie, who were heroes.

By all medical standards, Rodney should not have survived his astounding injuries. It bewilders doctors why he did not die on the scene or how he managed to stay conscious for as long as he did. Rodney should, by all means, be dead! It is with the grace of God, the quick actions of Sergeant Reiger and the amazing surgeons who acted to save Rodney; that he is with us today. He continues to shine in the medical world as a walking miracle.

Rodney: You really don't know how many lives you touch until you are involved in a critical incident yourself and people voice how you touched their life in one special way or another. Even the criminals and people I locked up personally voiced their concern.

The day of the attack, while Rodney was in surgery, his parents were told that "this case would never go to trial." The audacity it takes to confront a mother in the hospital; who is already facing the fact that her son may die, is the exact example of the shallowness that our legal system can stoop too, even when it is in regards to our law enforcement. Never mind the fact that an officer of the law, who was just trying to do his job was stabbed in such a cold, viscous and inhumane way. The fact that this mother and father were facing the possibility that the last time they saw their son alive just may be their final memory of him; none of that was even a concern.

There is a time and a place for everything and the hospital waiting room was not the place to drop a bomb like "this case will never go to trial." It's possible that the attorneys were trying to do their job, much like Rodney was trying to do that day, but is that a reason to confront a distressed mother in the emergency room in such an spiteful manner. When has "doing your job" become an excuse to act so callous to other human beings?

Allen Ford Hawkins was charged with Attempted Capital Murder of a Police Officer and was jailed pending trial. His father, David Hawkins, was a prominent Campbell County attorney and was good friends with William Petty (Lynchburg Commonwealth Attorney at the time). So, he was able to arrange for special prosecutors Paul Ebert and Jim Whillet to prosecute the case in court.

It was 18 months later the case went to trial and the controversy of sanity vs. insanity began. Hawkins was allowed to plead NOT GUILTY BY REASON OF INSANITY.

Even the judge was upset about having to accept his plea and apologized to Rodney and his family

Rodney described the trial as an "orchestration of the Special Prosecutor and the Defense Attorney AGAINST my will and request."

Hawkins was supposed to spend at least 8 years in a mental hospital before being eligible for public release. On November 6, 2002, after serving only 2 years and 11 months, Allen Hawkins was released, a FREE man with NO criminal history on his record.

Rodney: I was so angered by the outcome of the trial. I felt like I got cheated by the own system that I put my life on the line for every day. I lobbied, along with the widow of a slain police officer who was killed in the line of duty, who felt she had received the same treatment from the Commonwealth Attorney in another jurisdiction. We wanted to pass a law that Commonwealth Attorneys could not accept plea bargains without the full consent of the victim first. The first year we lobbied for this bill, it was killed. The second year – it became LAW!

Once Rodney was back on duty, he was assigned the position of School Resource Officer to give him time to recuperate. While he was there, he would seek out "problem children" and attach himself to them, in hopes of making a difference in their life. He knew these students needed him the most. He recalls meeting a student that was considered a "complete delinquent." He was being written up every day for offenses, such as, fighting, disrupting class and disrespect. Rodney made it a "professional goal to reach out to that child."

Rodney: I walked with him to class. I ate lunch with him. I participated with him during gym class. I assisted him on assignments. I stood with him and chatted with him while awaiting the school bus. I did this to make sure he had a constant presence in his life and to encourage him not to get into trouble. The year before he left the middle school and entered the high school, the young man indeed changed for the better. He was more respectful and was willing to offer a helping hand to others instead of slapping the hand that reached out to him. That teen is now an adult and often interacts with Rodney. "He always extends his hand to shake mine, we stop and talk, joke and continue a friendship that started seven years ago while he was a troubled middle school teen."

Rodney came a long way from the days he roamed the halls at Appomattox County High School. He was 16 years old when he first knew that he wanted to be a police officer. While participating in the program, "Leaders of Tomorrow," Rodney was assigned a mentor named, Bruce Eye, a Virginia State Police Special Agent. Bruce was chalk full of valuable information about law enforcement and Rodney seized every opportunity to learn from him. It was from Bruce's inspiration that Rodney wanted to be a cop!

After graduation he moved on to Central Virginia Community College where he earned an Associate's Degree in "Administration of Justice;" then on to Radford University where he earned a Bachelor of Science Degree in Criminal Justice. It was at Radford that he interned at the Appomattox County Sheriff's Office.

Rodney: My mentors were Sergeant Len Allen Smith and Investigator Wilson Staples. They showed me every positive and negative side to law enforcement. They really told me like it was. They taught me what opportunities were available for me. Investigator Staples is now serving his second term as sheriff of Appomattox County.

In July 1996, he accepted a position with the Campbell County Sheriff's Office as a Road Deputy and was enrolled in the Central Virginia Criminal Justice Academy. He was later made a Field Training Officer and Instructor. He was promoted to Master Deputy and served on the SWAT Team.

Four years after his near fatal afternoon with Allen Hawkins; Rodney was approached by the Bedford County

Sheriff's Office who offered him a position with their Internet Crimes Against Children Task Force (ICAC). Rodney took them up on their offer and made the move to Bedford County on February 1, 2003. He always believed that everything happens for a reason and was even more sure of that with ICAC! He knew in his heart that this was the work he was meant to do.

Rodney: The ICAC Task Force is a federally funded task force specifically designed to investigate the exploitation of children involving the Internet. There are 59 Task Forces nationwide and Bedford County was one of the first ten assigned in 1998.

In July 2006, he was promoted to Sergeant of the ICAC Unit. He worked on child pornography cases and he received the majority of his tips through the Cybertipline set up by the National Center for Missing and Exploited Children. He was a coordinator and supervisor for ICAC office in 57 police departments and sheriff offices throughout Virginia.

He participated in over 450 hours of training in the investigation of crimes involving computers and crimes against children. He holds an expertise in Child Pornography Investigations, Grooming and Profiling of a Sexual Predator and Education Outreach.

During Rodney's career, he received numerous outstanding recognitions including National Deputy of the Year Runner-Up in 1999, the Virginia Sheriff's Association Medal of Valor Award, the Campbell County Sheriff's Office Purple Heart Award, Military Order of Police Association Purple Heart Award and the National Sheriff's Association Purple Heart Award. In May 2008 Rodney received the "Law Enforcement Public Service Award," for his outstanding and dedicated public service to the nation and community which he he served. It was presented by the United States Attorney's Office Eastern District of Virginia.

He had a positive effect on many citizens who he came in contact with. One in particular was a little boy from a home of domestic violence. The police made numerous trips to the home and every time Rodney arrived their young son was in tears. Rodney, who had always been artistic, took that little boy under his wing and became his friend by drawing and coloring pictures for him. The boy proudly displayed the artwork on his bedroom walls.

It would be years later when Rodney would see the impact of his friendship. He was at a minor league baseball game when a man approached him with a wife and child at his side. It was that young boy from long ago! He recognized Rodney and wanted to introduce him to his family.

He told Rodney how he had gotten into some trouble growing up, but he was working hard putting his life back on track. He never forgot Rodney's visits and still had the pictures that he drew for him.

In October 2008, Rodney left the field of law enforcement for personal reasons. Though he continues to work in the field of Public Relations he has enjoyed traveling the new road that life has sent him on...that of the restaurant business. He is now a Front of the House Manager at Phase 2 Sports Bar. It's the spontaneity of life that is the driving force behind Rodney's days. Who knows, restaurant manager today and perhaps an author in his own write tomorrow!

*If a teen stated they wanted to follow in your chosen career path, what would be your advice for them?

Rodney: That a true police officer remains in their profession because it is "their" calling. You don't get into law enforcement for the money. You don't get into law enforcement to be a hero because your life can be taken away from you as quick as you pin on that badge and strap on the gun each day. I got into it for the adrenaline rush and "never" not knowing from one minute to the next what is going to happen. I have lived my "adrenaline" rush – I have experienced my HIGH of police work.

Detective Michael Laughland

When asked if he had ever been injured in the line of duty, the response from Detective Mike Laughland was simple.

Mike: Yes. Over the years I have had frequent flier miles at the local hospital. Most of them have been the occasional bumps and bruises from the unwillingness of the arrested person, IE resisting arrest. Many others were the pepper spray to the eyes.

Actually, he sustained more serious injuries than this. Murphysboro is a small town and after a year on the job he was still becoming familiar with the community and was only vaguely familiar with the smaller roads. When he received a call of disturbance at Hucks, the town's local convenience store; it would become anything but an ordinary call.

Once at the store he obtained the necessary information and drove to the suspects home. Upon arrival, he found himself on a dead-end road in a trailer park. The suspect greeted the officer by identifying himself as "the next President of the United States." Mike already knew that he was dealing with a "mentally deranged person." When Mike informed him that he was under arrest he resisted the officer. He even shouted that he was going back in his house to get his gun. Mike tried to keep him from re-entering the home, but he became combative which gave the officer no choice but to pepper spray him. Due to the wind direction, he also sprayed himself.

Mike: During the struggle I was pushed backwards off of the porch. Not a large fall but it was the lawn mower that was pushed under the deck that caused the problem. My foot caught under the middle cross bars and I fell backwards over the top handle. I was literally hanging. The thought of this guy coming out with a shotgun crossed my mind. I wiggled my way out of the position I was in while feeling the pain of a fractured ankle. I hobbled across the yard and took cover while calling for assistance.

He emerged from his home with a large black cylindrical object. Mike's eyes were still burning from the pepper spray. Things were all a blur, so he was not able to see for certain what he was holding. The subject spotted Mike's location and walked directly towards him. Mike drew his service weapon and ordered him to drop his object. He could tell that the subject was also dazed as he looked upon the officer and turned around and walked back into the trailer.

Today Mike believes that what made the suspect turn around was; hearing the police sirens of his back-up approaching. He made the right choice to turn around because in the decision of life or death things could have ended much worse. The man barricaded himself in his trailer for two hours. Mike credits a 30-year veteran Sergeant with the skills and know-how to be able to talk the subject out of the trailer without incident. The man served two years in a mental institution before being released. Today the man is respectful and pleasant towards Mike when they see each other in public. He has even grown to trust Mike and has often confided in him.

When Mike Laughland first became interested in law enforcement, he was a young boy, but he never suspected that he would one day choose it as his career. He graduated from high school in 1989 and enlisted in the Air Force for four years. The benefit of having a non-law enforcement job in the military is having a chance to do a one weekend tour of flight line patrol while the regular security force attended functions.

In the Air Force, Mike was assigned to a special group at Beale Air Force Base in California, where he built space suits for the U-2 and SR-71. He also taught Pilot Survival Training and maintained much of their survival equipment. He received an honorable discharge from the military in 1993 and began doing ride-alongs with the Yuba City California Police Department.

Mike: From then on, I knew exactly what I wanted to do. I really can't contribute my drive to do police work to anyone other than God himself. This is the place he had planned all along to use me. I just never knew growing up.

He went to college to earn his Emergency Medical Technician License. His first job as an EMT was with the Saline County Illinois Ambulance Service. He continued his college education and in 1995 he earned an Associate's Degree in Criminal Justice. He was hired as a patrol officer by the Murphysboro Illinois Police Department in March 1996 and continues to work for that department today. He transferred to the Investigations Department in April 2005 and was appointed the position of detective. He also works with the Jackson County Sheriff's Task Force doing drug and gun investigations. He has been trained in Death Investigations, Crime Scene Investigations, Cyber Crime Investigations and Crime Scene Photography.

In the summer of 2006, Mike was involved in a career case. He responded to an Armed Robbery at the Medicine Shoppe pharmacy. Two armed men stole a large number of narcotics and money. They did not have any suspects, but the robbery was picked up by the store's surveillance cameras.

Several weeks later those same two men and a third accomplice robbed a bank in a small town north of Murphysboro. Mike assisted the Jackson County Sheriff's Office in the investigation. They soon learned that these men were serial bank robbers and their crimes extended from Illinois into Indiana and Kentucky. On April 4, 2007 the men were caught.

It cannot be said enough that a police officer's job is one of the most unpredictable! Their calls range from false alarms, domestic disturbances, robberies and the more dangerous, life-or-death calls, involving shoot-outs. However, it's calls involving children that have always been particularly difficult for police officers because of the heart wrenching circumstances that the young impressionable children are forced into. They have to be careful as to not allow their over protective nature to cloud their perspective of the situation at hand. This was the case when Mike responded to a call for a child wandering in the streets of an unsafe neighborhood.

When Mike arrived, he found a toddler at the tender age of 18 months walking down the road, all alone. He certainly could not tell Mike his parents' names, his address or least of all his own name. Mike took him to the department and waited for anyone to arrive searching for a lost child. Shortly after, he noticed that the boy needed his diaper changed.

Mike: I was able to make a phone call and have a diaper delivered as well as some snacks and a drink in a sipper cup. With no one else to care for this child, and Children and Family Services one hour away, I fell into "mom mode." I changed the little man's pants and tried to care for him the best I knew how. Lucky for me, I had little ones at home, so nature took over.

The parents arrived approximately 2 1/2 hours later and were thankful to Mike for the care he gave their child. At this point, Mike switched back from "Mom Mode" to "Police Officer." He was furious with the duo and wanted to arrest them right then and there! However, he felt compassion for the child; knowing the last thing he needed was to be placed in the hands of strangers. Before he left the couple with the case worker, he explained what he COULD HAVE done to them and what their repercussions would be if this happened once more.

When he is off duty, Mike continues his work protecting the children, specifically on the Internet. Myspace and Facebook are popular sites for youth. Unfortunately, where there are children and teens; there will be predators, lurking in the shadows. These websites have been described by many as a "playground for predators." Mike works hard to help rid these sites of child molesters. He also teaches teens about hackers, spam and ways to protect themselves online. More importantly, he has made himself available to them for any of their concerns, whether it's harassment online, abuse, drugs or bullies in their everyday lives. He is not just a protector. He is their friend!

He encourages other police officers to be available to children and teens as well. Coming together with the youth, they have gone as far to have the teens add them to their "top friends list." Explaining that the motive behind this is that the predators will be less likely to contact teens who have cops as their top friends! A move that can best be described as BRILLIANT! Mike believes that LEW's should always work together whether they are in neighboring communities or on opposite sides of the world. It truly is a brotherhood and the "thin blue line" knows no boundaries.

Mike: I would like to see a Myspace wide directory in place and for all law enforcement to be verified by myspace. I would also like to see all ICAC Task forces across America to have a myspace profile. Just as "Tom" is a friend on every profile, I would like to see an ICAC Profile done the same way. This would give everyone someone to contact in case a predator should contact them. This would mostly apply to profiles of children but in some cases even adults.

*If a teen stated that they wanted to follow your chosen career path, what would be your advice for them?

Mike: I have offered many teens advice in this area, and for me it's always the same. Educate yourself the best you can, attend college after high school because you can't carry a handgun until you are 21 anyway, Military is always a good option for discipline and entering a team work mode, stay away from drugs and alcohol, and watch very carefully whom you associate with.

This article about Detective Laughland appeared in "The Southern" newspaper.

"Murphysboro police officers honored for work on murder case"

BY Adam Testa
THE SOUTHERN, Tuesday, March 11, 2008

MURPHYSBORO - Two Murphysboro Police Department employees received recognition from the city council for cracking a 17-year-old cold case murder last month.

Quincy Hughes of Murphysboro was arrested last month in connection with the 1991 murder of Cindy Lou Pavey in Murphysboro. Pavey had been found bludgeoned to death in her home while her children were in the other room of the house. With advances in forensics technology, Detective Michael Laughland and Deputy Chief Tim Legere reopened the case and found DNA evidence leading them to Hughes, who faces a preliminary hearing in Jackson County Circuit Court Friday.

Legere recommended the city council honor Laughland for his work on the case, and Mayor Ron Williams said the city council decided the deputy chief deserved to be honored as well. Laughland was presented with a plaque and a ribbon to wear on his uniform at Tuesday's council meeting.

Laughland's team attitude and desire to aid the department rather than himself played a crucial role in solving the case, Williams said. The mayor also said Laughland put his heart into the investigation and "didn't let it go."

Through partnerships and support with the U.S. District Attorney's office, the Jackson County State's Attorney's office, the Jackson County Sheriff's Department and the Murphysboro Police Department, the streets of Murphysboro continue to become a safer place, Williams added. "It's taking a part of this image we think is tainting us away," he said.

Tips for Children and Teens to Stay Safe When Using Social Networking Sites

1) Never post your personal information, such as cell phone number, address, or the name of your school.

2) Be aware that information you give out in blogs could also put you at risk of victimization. People looking to harm you could use the information you post to gain your trust. They can also deceive you by pretending they know you.

3) Never give out your password to anyone other than your parent or guardian.

4) Only add people as friends to your site if you know them in real life.

5) Never meet in person with anyone you first "met" on a social networking site.

6) Some people may not be who they say they are. Think before posting your photos. Personal photos should not have revealing information, such as school names or locations. Look at the backgrounds of the pictures to make sure you are not giving out any identifying information without realizing it. The name of a mall, the license plate of your car, signs, or the name of your sports team on your jersey or clothing all contain information that can give your location away.

7) Never respond to harassing or rude comments posted on your profile. Delete any unwanted messages or friends who continuously leave inappropriate comments. Report these comments to the networking site if they violate that site's terms of service.

8) Check the privacy settings of the social networking sites that you use: Set it so that people can only be added as your friend if you approve it. Set it so that people can only view your profile if you have

approved them as a friend.

9) Remember that posting information about your friends could put them at risk. Protect your friends by not posting any names, ages, phone numbers, school names, or locations. Refrain from making or posting plans and activities on your site.

10) Consider going through your blog and profile and removing information that could put you at risk. Remember, anyone has access to your blog and profile, not just people you know.

Tips for Families to Keep Their Children and Teens Safe Online

1) Discuss the dangers and future repercussions with your child.

2) Enter into a safe-computing contract with your child about his or her use of these sites and computer use in general.

3) Enable computer Internet filtering features if they are available from your Internet service.

4) Install monitoring software or keystroke capture devices on your family computer that will help monitor your child's Internet activity.

5) Know each of your child's passwords, screen names, and all account information.

6) Put the computer in a family area of the household and do not permit private usage.

7) Monitor what your child's friends are posting regarding your child's identity. Often children and their friends have accounts linked to one another, so it's not just your child's profile and information you need to worry about.

8) Know what other access your child has to computers and devices like cell phones and PDAs.

9) Report all inappropriate non-criminal behavior to the site through their reporting procedures.

10) Report criminal behavior to the appropriate law-enforcement agency including the NCMEC CyberTipline at www.cybertipline.com or the Internet Fraud Complaint Center at http://www.ic3.gov.

11) Contact your legislators and request stronger laws against Internet crime.

12) Visit the NetSmartz Workshop at www.NetSmartz.org for more information.

13) Remember that every day is Halloween on the Internet. People on the Internet are not always who they appear to be.

Corporal Richard C. Baudoin

Senior Patrolman Duane Carpenter

It can't be said enough that one aspect of a police officer's job is the unpredictability of it all! When Louisiana Officer Richard Baudoin received a call from his Shift Captain to bring a Voluntary Search Warrant to a city residence, he wasn't told upfront who they were looking for;

just to assist.

When he arrived, he was told they were searching for the fetus of a 14-year-old girl. She went to the hospital a few hours after delivery. She was bleeding and the told doctors and her parents that she gave birth 6 hours earlier. While doing an outside search of the home, Richard rummaged through the garbage can and found a towel soaked in blood. Feeling that lump of sadness catch in his throat he opened the towel and there was the baby! In Richard's eyes that was in deed a baby; not just a fetus. The events of the afternoon continue to haunt him.

For fellow Louisiana officer, Duane Carpenter, one of his moments of unpredictability came during a traffic stop. After handling the stop, he was walking back to his squad car and the vehicle, that he pulled over, attempted to rejoin traffic. But he drove into the path of an 18-wheeler, causing the truck driver to lose control. The truck flipped over and spilled a hazardous load of Tetra Hydrochloric Acid. Duane was able to pull the truck driver out of the wreckage and safely to the side of the road. For his heroic feat, Duane was awarded as Police Officer of the Year.

It all began for Richard when he was 13 years old and he attended a Father's Day Ceremony at his middle school. That afternoon changed the way he saw his own future. The father of a good friend of his was a guest speaker at the ceremony. As Richard listened to him talk about his job in law enforcement, his heart swelled with desire and honor in what being a police officer could do for his future.

He started working for the Crowley Police Department in 2000 and held positions in the traffic department, narcotics division and as a patrol officer. He credits Lieutenant Wayne Perry and his first shift supervisor, Lieutenant Berton Gauthreaux, for teaching him the skills he needs to know to do his job successfully. He was later promoted to Corporal with the Crowley Police Department in Louisiana.

Like Richard, Duane knew at a young age that he wanted to be a police officer. He was 13 when he joined the Junior Explorer Program and right away became active with members of the Louisiana Gonzales Police Department.

When he turned 21, he went into the police academy and upon graduation was stated a police officer for the Gonzales PD. He continues to serve there today and is now a Senior Patrolman. The Explorer Program has served as a boost for many officers in law enforcement.

Duane: The Explorer program shows young people the different aspects of Law Enforcement and gives you the chance to see what a Police Officer does on a daily basis. My biggest influence was Officer Robin Brunke, she watched over the Explorer Program and pushed each of us to do our best and follow our dreams of becoming a police officer. She served with the Police Department for approximately 25 years and just recently retired. She remains involved with the Police Department and Explorer Program even though she has retired.

Since his career began, Richard has been involved in numerous shoot outs. His squad car was once hit by a driver that ran through a stop sign causing his squad to be "t-boned." By the grace of God; Richard has escaped all of these incidents without serious injuries.

Duane has also been involved in several automobile accidents while on duty that have caused him to have lower back problems today. He has been able to avoid being involved in shoot-outs (knock on wood) but on January 5, 2008 while attempting to "unload an old rusty .22 caliber revolver" it shot off in his hand. The bullet went through his hand and ring finger and exited out through the knuckle. He had re-constructive surgery, which included removing a piece of bone from his arm and placing it in his finger. He returned to work a month later.

Sometime a police officer's job is just being in the right place at the right time! This was the case the day Richard observed a vehicle exiting a parking lot at such a high speed that when he went to make a right turn, he lost control of his car! The car flipped on its side and landed in a canal across from where Richard was parked.

Richard: I ran to the vehicle and jumped on the passenger side, which was pointing up now, opened the door and pulled the guy out of the vehicle, while still on my radio calling for help. The guy turned out to be Ralph Begnaud, famous Louisiana Comedian. He thanked me every day for saving his life.

When Richard was answering a domestic call in West Crowley, he noticed the fight had ensued into the front yard. He radioed the call in, then ran towards the duo in the fight, which he now realized was a man and a woman. Noticing the officer, the man pulled a knife from his back pocket. Richard pulled his asp and struck him on the right arm to knock the knife from his grip. Richard grabbed him and threw him to the ground while another officer handcuffed him. While they waited for the ambulance Richard administered first aid to the woman.

Richard: Upon asking her if this was her husband, she said no, that it was her ex-husband from California and he came down to kill her. Upon running his name on NCIC, it turned out he was wanted for 5 counts of Attempted 2nd Degree Murder in San Francisco. What a day!

Right before his eyes, a murder was about to take place. Due to quick thinking, the woman's life was saved. Officers have only seconds to decide the best course of action.

Richard had once noticed a youth who was headed down the wrong path in life and when the opportunity arose to jump in front of him, like Superman stopping a runaway train, he seized the chance! The youth was arrested for the first time when he was 10 years old and when he was 15 years old, he was still being arrested for numerous minor charges. Not wanting to see the young man end up in prison, he sat down with the mother and the two of them had a talk about options that were available.

He explained to the mother that the United States National Guard has a program for troubled youth. It is the

National Guard Challenge Program. It is geared towards youth ages 16-18. They teach life skills, as well as, citizenship, health and fitness, academic education, job skills and giving back to their community. It is a 22-week residential program that is followed by a year-long mentoring relationship with a specially trained member from each youth's community.

The mother was proud to enroll her son in the program and when it came time for him to work with a mentor, she asked Richard to do the part and he was glad to step up to the plate.

The young man was 17 years old when he completed the program and after that he joined the US Army ROTC program at the University of Louisiana. From there he enlisted in the United States Army. He is now a First Lieutenant and served a tour of duty in Iraq.

*If a teen stated that they wanted to follow in your chosen career path, what would be your advice for them?

Richard: First thing was Finishing School then College then look at where your life was from there, it might point to a different Direction.

Duane: If a teen wanted to become a police officer officer, I would encourage them to do it. I believe it is a Great job and I enjoy serving the city that I grew up in and where my family live. I would make sure the teen graduated high school, stayed out of trouble and followed their choice to be a police officer.

I dedicate "He's Always There" to Officer Richard Baudoin and Officer Duane Carpenter.

He's Always There

A call on the phone is a crying abused woman,
He has to try to save her from this violent man.
Rushing to the home, wonders if she will be alright,
Pulling in the driveway, he sees her under the light.

The very next day, a drug dealer is at a school,
Trying to get there is hard, and he has to keep his cool.
Wonder who he's selling to, if it's one of his own,
He arrives to the school and the drug deal is blown.

A car has overturned, and people are trapped,
He's on the way again, doesn't need the map.
He pulls beside the car, there are fumes from the gas,
He gets them all out just a minute before the blast.

A car goes flying by, the siren comes on once more,
How he hated these, he had done them so much before.
A nasty attitude and a mean look is what he got,
How people so hated to be pulled over by the cop.

But, he's always there, no matter what the time,
And though the pay is not good, he doesn't mind.
He'll save your children, and keep you safe and sound,
To serve and protect is what he has always vowed.

Sergeant Russ Aikman

On January 18, 2002, Sergeant Russ Aikman was getting dressed for work, on what started off as a seemingly normal day, until the power suddenly turned off. He was casually glancing outside to observe what was happening, when his minuter went off. A call came in concerning a Canadian Pacific Railway train that derailed between Burlington and Minot, North Dakota. Russ could tell by the tone of his voice that something else had gone terribly wrong.

He drove "Code 3" to the fire department and radioed his

whereabouts in to dispatch. They notified Russ that he was the first to respond. Due to the power failure the pager system was down. When Russ arrived at the station, he proceeded to call everyone on the roster using the land line phone. The police chief and fellow firefighters soon arrived.

The temperature that afternoon was -22 degrees. The train was carrying a load of anhydrous ammonia. This would turn out to be the largest ammonia spill that our country would ever see. Russ and fellow firefighters rushed from door to door to evacuate the neighboring homes. Meanwhile, one of the deputies was caught in the midst of the disaster and was calling out for help on the radio. It took firefighters and police officers six hours to locate the deputy who was then in a near death state.

Anhydrous ammonia is fatal when inhaled. It dries out the water in a person's body. Normally it would dissipate in the air, but the extremely cold temperatures caused it to form into a huge fog cloud that took over most of the city.

They worked tirelessly for 9 days running disaster operations. When the incident was over, one person was deceased and over 800 were treated with mild all the way to critical ailments. Russ developed a breathing ailment from the effects of the ammonia which to this day becomes aggravated from extremely humid temperatures or strenuous work. The brave members of the Fire, Police and EMS units were awarded the medal of valor by the mayor.

Russ got his first taste of law enforcement as a teen when he joined the Law Enforcement Explorer Group for Youth's that was sponsored by his community Sheriff's Department. In high school he participated in his school's, Vo-Tech EHOVE Career Center for Law Enforcement. He also volunteered as an instructor at the American Red Cross. Upon graduating from Danbury High School, he went on to Colorado Technical University where he earned an Associate's Degree in Criminal Justice. Yearning to learn as much as possible about law, he went on to Ohio's Bowling Green State University where he earned his Bachelor's Degree in Criminal Justice.

His career in law enforcement began in Cedar Point,

Ohio, where he served as a non-bonded (not certified) police officer. He went on to enlist in the Air Force as a Security Forces apprentice (military police for the Air Force). In the Air Force, he was a member of the Ward County Sheriff's Reserves and a volunteer firefighter EMT with the Burlington North Dakota Fire Department. He was promoted to SRT Team Lead (Situation Response Team) with the 91st SFS Squadron. He was deployed to the Kingdom of Saudi Arabia in 2001 and began his tour of duty to several countries.

In 2003, he received an honorable discharge from the Air Force and returned to his home town of Port Clinton, Ohio. He then went on to work as a firefighter EMT for the city. He joined their Hazardous Materials team and took on the job of an instructor for the American Red Cross.

One of the most heart wrenching moments in Russ's career happened when he answered a call for a male driver who lost control of his truck. The man over corrected a turn and shot across the street on a curve which caused his truck to roll several times. When Russ arrived, he surveyed the truck which was then upside down in a dry ditch, with the driver pinned to the cement viaduct. The driver was thrown through the windshield and was unconscious but breathing. Russ has never forgotten checking the man for a pulse and feeling the last beat of his heart.

The toxicology report determined that the man was driving 3x above the the legal limit and the autopsy report noted that he had torn his aorta. The aorta is the main artery that leaves the heart. Russ could have done to save him but at least the man did not have to die alone.

Russ: The doctors told me that he died very fast, which did not really help me feel better. The only thing worse than going to a fatal accident was having to notify the next of kin of the deceased. After this accident, I enrolled into EMT classes and joined the volunteer fire department.

In 2006, he moved to Wellington, Ohio where and took on the position of Reserve Police Officer and EMT with Lifecare EMS. He worked for Mosley Investigations in Columbus

Ohio as a private police and investigations officer. He then moved on to Columbus where he worked as an Investigator and now Sergeant. He continues to work as a Reserve Officer with the Wellington Police Department.

The ongoing training that officers receive is vital to performing their job. Their quick thinking and response techniques is what they utilize to stay alive and keep safe. Once while Russ was escorting a mental patient in the back of an ambulance the subject started fighting with him and the EMT. The ambulance attempted to come to a stop and slowed to a speed of 15 MPH. The man then opened the back door and tried to shove Russ out of it. As Russ fell to the ground, he grabbed hold of the subject to keep him from escaping. They fell to the side of the road and slid down into a muddy ditch where a fight ensued. The startled officers in the police cruiser behind the ambulance brought their car to a screeching halt and raced to assist Russ.

Russ: This guy had committed a violent stretch of crimes and no one wanted to see him get away. In the struggle as the other two police officers parked the cruiser and came down to the ditch to assist me, I had injured my left knee. I was off duty for four months and had two surgeries on the knee. I spent another three months on light duty in dispatch before returning to regular patrol work.

The reality of how unpredictable police work can be struck Russ one night while he was working at a haunted house event, known as, "The Haunted Hydro," He was watching crowds of people enter the park when he noticed a couple, in their 20's, standing approximately 12 feet from him. The male was grabbing hold of the female as she fell to the ground.

He rushed to the couple as the man continued to hold onto the female who was now passed out on the ground. He radioed for EMS and checked the female for a pulse, but she wasn't breathing. The park's staff retrieved his trauma bag and oxygen bag from his cruiser. He and staff members began rescue breathing, as a deputy arrived with an AED unit that they quickly applied to the patient. Russ was

114

relieved after the third round of CPR and shocks enabled her to regain a pulse. EMS crews arrived shortly after and transported her to the hospital.

Russ: It was the greatest feeling in the world to find out that we saved this woman's life. Four of us were awarded the Extraordinary Personal Lifesaving Award by the National American Red Cross. The greatest moment of this whole situation happened when the woman's family thanked me for "Giving their daughter back to them for one more Christmas." Sadly, 8 months later the woman died of massive heart failure. It felt great knowing that I was able to give the family one more holiday with her.

His compassion for keeping his community safe is what motivates him to serve on each branch of the protective services field, as an officer, firefighter and EMT.

Russ: I have been awarded many certificates, medals and such over my career. I can honestly say that not once have I ever done something wanting, thinking about or expecting any kind of award. It is nice to be honored for saving someone's life, however I would not have changed one thing about the care, service or professionalism I exhibit during my tenure in Public Safety. There really are too many calls to remember everyone, but I do recall every fatal accident I have ever worked. It is strange how the mind functions, recalls and works. I can remember the names, details, locations of every fatal accident, yet I cannot begin to fathom every ticket or traffic stop I have made. With that being said, I urge anyone that has gone through a rough time or call to seek help. It does no one any good to bottle emotions up inside and never let them out. After fatal accidents or traumatic situations there are debriefings held to help officers cope with the stress of the situation, so please, don't be afraid to talk to someone about it because you are not alone.

Russ worked on several independent films as a technical

adviser for Law Enforcement and Emergency Medical Services. He has had cameo appearances in films as a police officer and in "The Rapture" he appeared as a bailiff.

*If a teen stated that they wanted to follow in your chosen career path, what would be your advice for them?

Russ: My advice for a teenager that is interested in this career would be stay in school. I know that is cliché, but it is the truth. Do well in high school and go to college. If you have a choice, DON'T GO INTO THE MILITARY. I did learn a lot as a military member, but if I could do it again, I would say go to college and get a degree. Then, after being a graduate, you can go into the military as an Officer. This pays a lot better, has many opportunities that are much better than going in as an enlisted person. Lastly, in today's world, a degree is almost as necessary as speaking Spanish or Arabic. I have learned Spanish and am working on learning Arabic. If someone is truly interested in Law Enforcement, having special skills such as being bi or tri lingual, would help out greatly. One other thing remember that anything you put online is public knowledge and as a police officer you are held to a higher standard than most citizens.

Sergeant David William Childress

There are people in this world simply driven by pure anger, beer muscles or drug abuse and these people will fire at the police simply to resist going to jail. Sergeant David Childress learned this lesson in February 1974 when he and several officers were involved in a shoot-out with, 18-year-old, Mark Anthony Terry. David was shot between the eyes during the altercation and the pellet remains in his forehead to this day. An inch to the left or right and David would have been blinded.

The police are not going to surrender to a subject with a gun. Shooting at the police is not a solution to legal problems and will only add up to more charges, a longer sentence and higher fines. In the worst-case scenario, it can result in the death of the subject at large or the police officer's death.

Though David has suffered several injuries on-duty; he considers them all a part of the job. His last on-the-job injury was life threatening; the worst he ever encountered. On November 15, 2003, a driver went through a red light and crashed into his police vehicle. He took off the entire front of his squad car. David was unable to work for a month and continues to have neck and back pain today.

For the most part, police work is a thankless job. Officers like David do what they do for the love of their work. The chance to help people, to rescue people and rid the streets of dangerous people; to protect the innocent is the only reward they seek. There are times when the police do have an opportunity to learn that their efforts have made a difference.

One of the men David arrested for drinking and driving later confronted him because he wanted to thank him. He told David it was his arrest that was the scare he needed to straighten out his life. Another time that David was confronted was during a dinner date with his wife. A man he once pulled over for speeding approached David and said, "You're the cop who stopped me the other day, I just wanted to thank you again for not writing me a ticket." He mentioned to his wife how nice David was during the stop. Showing a little kindness does go a long way!

For one afternoon when he was off duty but still in uniform; David noticed a teenage girl who appeared to be extremely sad and down. She approached David and struck up a conversation. The compassionate officer inside of him needed to find out what was wrong and what he can do to help her. He learned that she was deeply depressed and didn't feel that she had anything to live for.

Dave: I spoke with her about life and stuff and told her about Christ. She was very receptive. Her friend came back out of

the restroom (another girl) and I talked with her as well.
When they left, she seemed to be much better.

In this situation he will never know if his kind words made a difference with the young girl, he was simply glad to be there at the time she needed someone. Perhaps it was the fact that he was in uniform that made him approachable to the young lady. So often, people just need someone to listen to them. Once again, he said it is just a part of being a police officer.

When David was 19 years old, he married his high school sweetheart (one day after graduation). His first priority: A JOB! During his job hunt, Barry, his cousin (through marriage) was working as a police officer with the Richmond Bureau of Police and he was the first to suggest a career in law enforcement to David. He coaxed David into applying for a position as a Police Cadet.

After a long career with the Bureau, Barry was later forced to retire due to severe back injuries suffered while on duty.

David: When he retired, he was one of our Forensic Officers and one of the best in Virginia. He was a "CSI" person before anyone knew what CSI was all about.

David's career in law enforcement officially began on July 1, 1968. That was the beginning of a long fulfilling career in law. He went on to the Police Academy and graduated in November 1969. He was made an Acting Sergeant in January 1976 and on to Sergeant on December 2, 1978. He learned (by example) early on about how to work with fellow officers.

David: A Sergeant I had was being yelled at by another officer prior to the start of Roll Call. The Sergeant, instead of jumping up and bitting the officer's head off, said to him in a very claim voice, "If you have something to discuss, let's go back to my office and discuss it." I always remembered that moment and tried to be the same way.

David served the Richmond Police Department for 40 years and was President of the Richmond Coalition of Police. He has since retired his position as a Sergeant. He has worked in almost every division in the department and was the only officer to serve as the Risk Management Officer.

How he became the "Risk Management Officer" is an interesting event itself. It started when a fellow officer wrote a letter to the local newspaper; praising the police chief and how he ran the department. David, however, knew most of the letter was filled with falsities and the reason behind the letter was that the officer was bucking for a promotion. This didn't go over well with David who carried the same values inside of him as the famed New York Police Officer, Frank Serpico, and that was honesty and integrity above all! David responded to the letter and several days afterwards it was published; much to the dismay of the police chief but in awe of fellow officers who told David that he had a set of "brass balls" for writing that letter.

Sure enough, retaliation was in order for him! A week after his letter appeared in the paper, he received a transfer order. Effective the following Saturday, David was being relocated to the Office of Professional Standards (Internal Affairs) as the department's new "Risk Management Officer." However, when he showed up for work no one really knew what he was supposed to do.

He wasn't issued an office or any equipment. After a quick search through the building they found a small room that he could use and then brought in a filing cabinet, a desk and a couple of chairs. It would take several more days to get a computer and a phone for him.

David: Major Frank Monahan had some ideas of what he wanted me to do as the "Risk Management Officer." He explained what he wanted, and I started working on his directions. What they had me do was to compile records on all Police Vehicle Accidents and Police Pursuits and to do monthly reports to the Command Staff. A couple weeks after I was made the Risk Management Officer, the Department's "Safety Officer" was transferred under my supervision. The Safety Officer was a civilian who received all police employee injury reports and followed up on them. So, through him, I also became involved in all police employee injuries. Another thing I did while in this position was to assist in the revision of several of the Department's General Orders (formerly known as Standard Operating Procedures).

I fully believe that they (certain members of the Administration) were hoping that I would just totally fail in the position of being the Risk Management Officer. But, instead, I succeeded in everything they wanted me to do, plus some.

David (and the department's computer expert) created several computer data bases in MS Access. He is also responsible for reinstating the Department's "Accident Review Board" and sat as a permanent member on the Board for monthly review of all police vehicle accidents.

The name of which has since been changed to the "Risk Management Review Board." When Chief Jerry Oliver transferred to a new department, he was replaced by Chief, André Parker. Shortly after that David was transferred once more. He went back on the street as a Shift Sergeant in the 4th Precinct. The position of "Risk Management Officer" has since been abolished.

He still carries with him all of the good and bad of his days as a police officer. He clearly remembers everything from traffic control, to training fellow officers, to counseling teens, and even investigating homicides. His worst case was investigating the death of a 16-year-old and having to step over his brain matter at the crime scene.

Today David is an avid collector of law enforcement memorabilia. He has accumulated thousands of law enforcement patches from all over the world! His collection is also compiled of numerous badges, uniform hats, ball caps, T-shirts, lapel pins, and all sorts of law enforcement related items.

*If a teen stated that they wanted to follow in your chosen career path, what would be your advice for them?

David: The job of being a police officer is not just a 'job', it is a 'calling'. You have to get into the profession because you have a desire to help, not just for the 'thrill' of chasing bad guys, which is a lot a fun. But, being a law enforcement officer is very demanding. It is hard on your family life. It is hard on you. To be a cop, you must be willing to sacrifice a lot. There are things that you can't (or at least shouldn't) do as a cop. There are times, important times, that you will miss in your family's life. You have to want to be a cop for the possible good that you can do and not for any rewards you may get, cause there won't be any. Being a cop is a way of life.

I am the Officer

I have been where you fear to be.
I have seen what you fear to see.
I have done what you fear to do.
All these things I have done for you.

I am the one you lean upon.
The one you cast your scorn upon.
The one you bring your troubles to.
All these things I have been for you.

The one you ask to stand apart.
The one you feel should have no heart.
The one you call the "man in blue."
But I am a person, just like you.

And through the years,
I have come to see,
That I am not what you ask of me.

So take this badge. Take this gun.
Will you take it? Will anyone?

And when you watch a person die,
And hear a battered baby cry,
Then do you think that you can be,
All these things you ask of me?

Patrolman Joseph McKenney

Patrolman Joseph McKenney is the only officer in Hazard County, Kentucky to receive three Meritorious Life Saving Awards. The first came in December 2005 when he responded to a call for a 19-year-old who overdosed and stopped breathing. He performed CPR and resuscitated her before EMS arrived. The second was in April 2008 when he became a lifesaving link for a woman in need of EMS care that was seven minutes away. Seven minutes is a long time for a person who has stopped breathing...too long!

Joe: A 64year old woman called 911 saying she was smothering. I responded (I always responded on EMS calls in my patrol area) and saw her slumped over in her chair through the window. I forced the door open and checked, and she had no pulse and was not breathing. I did CPR for about 7 minutes before EMS arrived (they were extremely busy) and then rode in the ambulance with them to the hospital and before reaching the hospital we were able to restore a pulse.

He earned his third award in 2008 when responding to a call about a shoplifter at Wal-Mart. When Joe attempted to arrest the suspect, he resisted, and a struggle ensued. The subject grabbed a pair of scissors and attacked Joe. In the fight the man stabbed himself in the heart which also caused his lung to collapse. Joe performed immediate first aid and saved the subject's life. It was during those times that Joe was reminded he has a purpose in law enforcement and in this world as a whole! He carries the strong belief that every call he responds to is important.

Joe: I think the entire general public influences me because I put my badge on everyday knowing what could happen to me at work, but when I know people are able to spend more time with their family that they may have not been able to, had I not been there, that's my influence, motivation, and where I draw my dedication from.

He worked his first job in public services when he was a senior in high school. He completed his EMT training and went to work as a volunteer firefighter with Viper Fire and Rescue. He moved from Viper, Kentucky to Ohio to attend paramedic school where he then worked as an EMT for five years. He got his bump in law enforcement with the Montgomery County Sheriff's Office in Dayton Ohio and the Ohio State Highway Patrol. He returned to Kentucky upon hearing that his mother fell ill and on August 1, 2005, he went to work for the Hazard Police Department as a Sergeant. He has since retired from the police department and now works as a Registered Nurse.

With continuous changes and new findings in law enforcement, police officers often take advantage of opportunities to further their education. Joe is an officer who doesn't only seize the opportunity to further his education he also educates and trains other officers.

Some of his certifications include:

Certified Taser International Instructor
International Association of Chiefs of Police Drug Recognition Expert
Expert Marijuana Analyst
Nationally Registered Emergency Medical Technician
Pressure Point Control Tactics Self Defense Instructor

He has sustained several painful injuries while on duty. In October 2006, while attempting to arrest a shoplifter at Walmart he was once again attacked. The subject sliced him with a box cutter razor blade.

One of his worst injuries happened in March 2007. He answered a domestic violence call and the man attempted to flee the scene, starting a foot chase with Joe close behind him. While he chased the suspect through the mountains he stepped in a hole, which caused him to fall and break his leg. He later found out that he tore both menisci in his left knee. Amazingly enough, the fall and the broken leg did not keep this officer down. Within seconds he was back on his feet continuing the chase. He ran for another quarter mile and apprehended him before any other help arrived.

Joe knew he needed to get this abuser off of the streets before anyone else was hurt. He did not think of the pain he was in from the broken leg; his adrenaline rushed through him and nothing was going to stop him from the pursuit. Viper, Kentucky was proud to have such a dedicated officer protecting their streets. Before you criticize the work of the police ask yourself this question: Would you chase down an abuser knowing that you are running on a broken leg?

Police work is a desire that people are born with and is extremely gratifying to those wearing the badge. Much like the excitement an athlete feels when they play in sporting events, so is the excitement and happiness that law enforcement workers feel everyday being able to protect and serve for their community.

People in the community would often thank Joe (even when he was off duty) for his actions as an officer. His parents have been told by people how thankful they are for things that Joe has done and has been a part of to help them feel safe in their city.

*If a teen stated that they wanted to follow in your chosen career path, what would be your advice for them?

Joe: I would tell them to be prepared for anything and everything, because no matter what, when you think you've seen it all, something else comes along. Also, I've seen my fair share of heartache and pain in this career, but you've got to be able to take the bad and learn from it and take the good and cherish it.

Chief Stacey White

Chief Stacey White will never forget the day his department responded to the Oklahoma City bombing of the Alfred P. Murrah Federal Building. It was on April 19, 1995 that Timothy McVeigh blew up the Murrah Building in Oklahoma City by planting a bomb inside a Ryder moving van and leaving the vehicle parked in front of the building.

The bomb exploded at 9:02 AM, the time when many were arriving for work. There were 168 people killed and hundreds more injured. There was a daycare center on the bottom floor and with great sadness, 19 children were killed in the blast. Stacey and his officers were among the first who responded and stayed to assist throughout the ordeal. They were responsible for the security of the inner perimeter around the building and also security for some of the evidence found in the building. With a heavy heart, they worked effortlessly to assist in the removal of survivors and recovery of victims. The images from that day continue to haunt Stacey.

Stacey: I was moved by the togetherness of the Oklahoma people. Even during their pain, the families of the fallen victims came around and pinned angel pins on all of us who were participating in the recovery mission, a very emotional moment. Some of those people were family members of children who were lost in the bombing.

As challenging as it may be for the police to keep their work separate from their home environment; it becomes all the more difficult to do when children are involved on calls. Stacey is no stranger to these feelings and has taken steps to repair the lives of children he comes in contact with.

He was driven to help children upon seeing how disheveled their lives became when their parents were taken to jail and they, the truly innocent, were left behind with foster parents. Some of which showed very little love and compassion for the children in their care. Unfortunately, we live in a time when older children have almost no chance of being adopted. Imagine the ache in a child's heart when they have nowhere to call home; no parents or families there to celebrate the holidays; no one to discuss the events of their school days and no one to share their worries, fears, goals and victories.

Stacey felt the desire to help children in those situations. He and his wife have since adopted four children and have a fifth foster child. Though their foster child was never legally adopted she is no less a part of his family than the others. Stacey stands by the statement that she is just as much "his child" as the rest of the children in their home and will always be his "daughter." His three son's Trey, Dreyce and Marquis came to his home as foster children after their mother was arrested and jailed on drug charges. It was several years later when they were allowed to adopt them.

He adopted his daughter, Shelby, under similar situations. His daughter, Devon, was taken in when her parents broke up and they asked Stacey and Shannon if they can raise her. Stacey and Shannon know they cannot change the world as a whole but they also know that their corner of the world will be a better place for all that they have done.

His biggest influence and role model was John Wayne. It was his patriotic tones and dedication to our country that he admires and tries to live up to every day. During the 2008 election year, Stacey was disappointed at how petty the politicians acted toward each other, when there are more important concerns in this country.

He would like to see Americans stand up and be American, not Republican, not Democrat, not Independent, just plain old Americans.

Stacey: I've seen what happens here in the line of duty, those who work in this type of career know what we are to face, in most cases we are prepared to deal with our jobs. One thing we are not prepared to deal with is the hypocritical politicians who are more concerned about slandering each other's images over party line differences rather than thinking about the hardships our men and women in uniform face day to day.

Stacey is a 1985 graduate of Bixby High School and from there he enlisted in the Marines where he worked as an infantryman with the 2nd Battalion 7th Marines for three years. He was then transferred to Quantico, Virginia where he was an instructor for the Marine Corps Combat Development Command. It is there that marines learn warfare techniques and battle strategies. They also develop and test weapons and educate the marines in the fields of doctrine, organization, training and education, material, and leadership.

It was while serving in Camp Pendleton, California, that he met a young lady named, Shannon. She was originally from Scotland and it wasn't long after meeting Stacey that she won over his heart and would become his bride. The two are still together today.

He was honorably discharged from the Marines in 1990 and began his career in law enforcement after that. His first experience was working as a Reserve Deputy in Virginia. He has since served as an investigator, patrol officer, shift supervisor, mounted patrol coordinator and drug task force member. He is now Chief of Police for Oklahoma's Kiefer Police Department. He credits local Bixby Police Officers, Floyd Simmons, Richard Johnson and Walter Birdsong for inspiring him to become the officer that he is today.

Some of his more difficult moments as an officer were brought on from weather emergencies. As a deputy at the Pawnee County Sheriff's Office, Stacey and a Corps of Engineer Park Rangers rescued a family stranded on a sinking boat during a severe thunderstorm on Lake Keystone. Armed with only a rescue boat; they battled severe wind and rain and hoped that lightning didn't strike their "metal" boat in the process. Police work may be seen as a "thankless job" but there is a family in Pawnee County that will always be thankful for the brave officer who rescued their family.

In 2005, during a tornado, Stacey suffered injuries when his patrol car was blown from the roadway into a ditch. He continued to patrol throughout the storm; knowing it was his duty to make sure the citizens of their community safely reach shelter.

He once suffered minor lung damage while helping an elderly couple escape from a burning house. Even though police officers do not have the protective gear that fire fighters carry; that does not stop them from entering a burning building when someone's life is at risk.

Human life holds such a sacred value to Stacey that no matter what the situation; he does his best to achieve a positive outcome. Such as the day he responded to a call for a male trying to commit suicide. As chief negotiator, Stacey spent two hours of extremely tense deliberation convincing the man to hand over his gun and seek psychological help. It was a difficult call but well worth it in the end.

Stacey: A sad note, a supervisor and good friend of mine died in the line of duty just after midnight on the 29th of May 2008. Sgt Les Wilmott was involved in an auto accident which took this 54-year-old husband and father away from his family and ended a 33-year career in law enforcement.

During his career, Wilmott served as a Patrolman at Jenks Police Department, a Chief of Police for Inola and Beggs Police Departments and an Instructor, Teacher and Commander with the Kiefer Police Department. His influence in law enforcement was felt everywhere. Officers that worked with Sgt. Wilmott have called him "a Rock" of man who has always been there to help anyone who needed help and ready to stand against anyone willing or attempting to harm another.

The Oklahoma law enforcement community lost a great man who made such an impact on so many fellow Officers that his legacy will live on for generations to come.

He was a loving father and husband who was dedicated to his family. They were the most important things in life to Les and it shows when you see the love shared by each of them, all the way down to his grandchildren. His sons Jake and Matt have begun following in their Dad's footsteps, Jake currently serving in Law Enforcement and Matt looking to start a career in Law enforcement.

INFORMATION ON LES WILMOTT HAS BEEN USED WITH PERMISSION FROM THE KIEFER POLICE DEPARTMENT WEBSITE. THEY MAINTAIN ALL COPYRITES AND PERMISSION FROM THE DEPARTMENT IS REQUIRED FOR FURTHER USE.

*If a teen stated that they wanted to follow in your chosen career path, what would be your advice for them?

Stacey: Get a college education and always shoot for higher goals and improvement of yourself. Integrity is the most important thing a Police Officer has.

"Our Fallen Brother" is a tribute to Officers, like Sergeant Les Wilmott

Our Fallen Brother

As I held him close, I began to cry
Wondering and hoping our friend would never die
I could see the whites of his eyes, as he held me tight
The wind whisked through his hair, as we saw the light

He cried no more as we fell to the ground
His one single tear, would never be found
Cry not my friend God will take you home
The Angels in Heaven will not be alone
You're safe and well as a child to his mother
You will always be remembered as
OUR FALLEN BROTHER

Sergeant Bill Reinert

Police Officer Scott Flowers

As Police Officers and Christians, Sergeant Bill Reinert and Officer Scott Flowers seize opportunities to use their position as cops to counsel citizens to change their lives for the better.

Scott: I HOPE that I affect someone every time I'm on duty and I'm not just saying that. If I didn't care about the difference I made with people, I'd be doing something else making more money and seeing my family more. I really can't say when I've walked away thinking I really affected someone in a positive way. Unfortunately, that's a thing that we don't usually see or hear about. The only feedback we usually get is negative in the form of complaints.

Bill's first chance to make a difference in someone's life came when he arrested a juvenile for breaking into homes and stealing. He brought him in using the "bad cop" tactics. He knew that this was his chance to not only find out the truth about the break-ins but to help turn this boy around and send him down the better road. He was sure to interrogate him in front of his parents (who were aware of Bill's agenda to "scare him straight") and within two hours the boy was crying and confessed.

Another chance Bill found to help change a citizen's life

for the better came during a domestic violence call. The husband beat his wife and put her head through the wall; causing her to receive multiple stitches from her injuries. There was blood everywhere in the house! It was one of the worst scenes Bill had come across in his career. The husband fled the scene before the police arrived and was on the run for eight days. During that time, Bill counseled the wife and was able to suede her into leaving the husband and seek help for herself and her children. Without Bill's support one can only imagine what her life would have become. The first step for an abused woman is to make her decision to leave; it is also the most difficult step for them to take...a seemingly impossible one, if there is no one to encourage them.

Victims of abuse aren't just beaten down physically but emotionally as well. Sometimes what they need the most is someone from the outside to come in and encourage them. They need someone to raise their heads and make them aware to the fact that they have self-worth and deserve a better life.

Bill has recently started the "Praise and Worship" Facebook page; serving as a positive role model not only to his community but to people across the country!

For several years, Scott has worked as a director in the ministry of a Christian Camping and Conference Center at the Camp Oak Hill and Retreat Center. The camp is based out of Raleigh, North Carolina and began as a "dream" of business and community leaders. They resurrected remnants of an old school into the Camp Oak Hill that stands today. The counselors encourage teens to live every aspect of their life to the fullest. Camp Oak Hill is proud to serve as a place where dreams are made, self-esteem is lifted, and lifelong bonds are formed

Every police officer experiences that one call that changes the way they carry out their job. For Scott it came when he was a rookie and he answered a call for a traffic accident. A tractor trailer had T-boned a small Saturn and Scott was the first person on the scene.

Scott: There were two subjects trapped inside the car (front passenger and rear passenger). The front passenger had the front grill of the semi on top of him and his head was pretty bashed in. The rear passenger was just screaming. All I could see was all this carnage, smoke and screams and my first thought was "someone call 911!" The scariest part was when I realized that that was me. The driver of the Saturn was 19 and was well intoxicated. Because of her, her passenger was dead, and it struck me how stupid it was. That call motivates me every time I deal with a drunk driver.

One of Bill's more tense calls happened when a female ran a gate on a Navy Base while holding a knife to her 18-month-old baby. When Bill arrived at the scene, she was on the flight line. It was when she noticed Bill and his partner that the car chase began.

His partner was on foot and Bill was in his squad car. When Bill caught up with her, he jumped from his car with his gun drawn. She was still in her vehicle at this time and quickly sped off once more. In seconds he was back in his car and proceeded to chase her. He caught up to her quickly as they sped around the corner at 60mph. The chase quickly came to an end when she wrecked her vehicle into the double doors of a restaurant.

Bill: Another patrolman joined me with guns drawn and we got her to exit the vehicle. She was using the baby as a shield, so I could not get a clear shot except for a head shot. All along we were yelling at her to drop the knife. I didn't want to take a head shot because of where the bullet might have gone.

With the baby's life in danger; the situation was becoming a desperate one. Bill's watch commander had a clear shot for her leg and he took it. With that they were able to rush up on her and take the baby from her arms. Later at the hospital they learned that she was under the influence of drugs.

It was when Bill was in elementary school that he knew he wanted to be a cop and told his parents his dream. It was watching the police in his hometown of Amarillo, Texas that inspired him; particularly a motor cop affectionately named "Chocolate Chip." He showed Bill the bright side of law enforcement; the good they do for a community and the positive impact they have on citizens. All of this was a motivator for Bill.

Throughout his career he worked as a Field Training Officer, Bike Unit Cop and Watch Commander. Recently he has taught an Emergency Vehicle Operators Course (EVOC) and Non-Lethal Weapons training (NLW), which contains OC Spray, baton, handcuffing, and hand to hand combat. After serving as a Sergeant with the Blount Island Police Department he transferred to the Jacksonville Sheriff's Office. With Jacksonville he has an opportunity to further his career in law enforcement. It's here that he feels at home and plans to retire.

Scott's interest was always with the military. Unfortunately, he was turned away due to having diabetes. He had friends who were police officers and they filled him with stories about their on-the-job experiences and took him for ride-alongs.

However, Scott is the son of a police officer and as he watched his dad serve the public as a police officer, he "knew" that he wanted to do anything in his life EXCEPT become a cop.

Still, he was never satisfied with a desk job. He is an adrenaline junkie and the idea of a career in law enforcement was becoming more appealing to him with every ride along that he participated in with his cop friends. When he became a cop himself; it filled that part of him that desired the military lifestyle and enabled him to interact with the public.

His first job in law enforcement came in 2001 with the Wayne County Sheriff's Office in Goldsboro, North Carolina. He also served on the patrol division for the Mount Airy Police Department and from there he went on to work for Chapel Hill Police. He remains with the CHPD as a PO3 (similar to senior officer) on General Patrol.

He has been in quite a few chases and fights from people

resisting arrest. There is not much that can stop him from bringing in a suspect. Once during a hard scuffle, the man fought fist to cuff with Scott to try and escape the clutches of the officer. Scott was not about to give in, however, Scott did injure his back in the fight. The subject's attempts to keep from going to jail were futile and only added to his charges later. Unfortunately for Scott, he still suffers pain from those injuries that day.

Another serious injury came during a foot chase to catch a purse snatcher. Scott fell and received a deep gash on his knee. He jumped back to his feet and continued the chase until he caught the thief. Later that night, he received 10 stitches on his knee.

His most traumatic experience came the night he was called to rescue a young man who drown in a swimming pool. He was trying to rescue a friend who could not swim and became succumbed by the waters himself. Scott performed CPR while he prayed for EMS to arrive, so they can take over. He was unable to resuscitate the man and the memories from that afternoon continue to follow him today.

Scott: I still can see the kid's face and it woke me up for days right after that.

*If a teen stated that they wanted to follow in your chosen career path, what would be your advice for them?

Bill: I would tell them that it is a very dangerous career and that it is not for the weak hearted. I would also tell them that it is a great career and I get a lot of enjoyment from helping people in need.

Scott: Make sure that this is what you want to do because what you see on TV is only a small fraction. it doesn't show the boring part of the job. There's things you see that you never wanted to see, smells you never wanted to smell, and you see the worst in people. After all this you have to go home and be "normal" for the sake of your sanity and your family, kinda tough, especially for just a little pay. But, if you do still want to do the job, realize that the choices you make now affect the candidate that you will be later for employment. meaning, make dumb choices now and you have to bring them up and answer for them when you're trying to get sworn and hired.

I would like to dedicate the poem, "When a Cop Sleeps," to Officer Scott Flowers and Sergeant Bill Reinert.

When a Cop Sleeps

Sometimes when a cop sleeps, the demons come. The demons bring all the things they want to forget. The demons bring the tears and sweat, the spit and the blood.

The demons bring the broken bodies from the wrecks; the sickening smell of death and the kids. Oh God, not the kids. Mainly the demons bring the eyes. The hatred and desperation in the eyes of the people they fight.

The pleading and pain of the people they try to help and the quiet and blankness in death of the ones they couldn't.

The demons bring sounds too. The sounds of tires skidding and metal crunching from the wrecks. The gunshots that seem so loud on TV yet so muffled on the street. The screams and crying that all blend together after a while.

The demons won't leave. Alcohol and sleeping pills work for a while but they come back.

Some have used their own deaths to flee from them, but most of us are scared that in causing our own death...we'll be with them forever.

But the demons aren't all that bad. It's better for the demons to come in your sleep, than for the angels to come during your shift, (They say that if you're time comes on the job, your fallen brothers come back to take you home).

So the next time you see a cop having a bad day who he seems irritated and you think, "What a jerk!" Stop for a moment and wonder: What demons came to him last night or what new ones did he meet today?

Patrolman Christopher J. Veze

Have you ever called the police and wondered WHY it took them so long to arrive? Well, one obstacle that delays the police are other drivers on the road. There are drivers who refuse to yield to police officers who are trying to do their job. They lack the common courtesy to even slow down for a squad car with full lights and sirens blaring and many times; will also try to cut them off. This scenario became all too surreal for Patrolman Chris Veze.

Chris was responding to a domestic violence call when his cruiser was struck on the side by a delivery truck. The driver was negligent to the fact that Chris had his lights and sirens on and proceeded forward, actually expecting Chris to move from his path. The police cruiser was totaled but there was no damage to the delivery truck.

That incident serves as an example of a time when a woman needed the police to rescue her from a dangerous situation and help was delayed because of a careless driver.

Chris: I had minor injuries consisting of muscle strains and was back to work the next shift. I have been very tactical throughout my career and situations have worked out for the best. Our training plays a vital role in how an Officer reacts to such incidents and circumstances. Fight or flight.

The next time you see police officers traveling at a high rate of speed; it is because someone needs their help! Let them do their job! If it was you or your child who needed help; would not you want other drivers on the highway to yield so that the officer could come to aid?

Chris has known, in his heart, since he was six years old that he wanted to be a cop. In fact, it was then that he told his mom and dad of his dream.

Chris: As I grew up, I always had a profound respect and compassion for all people. I did some stupid things as a kid and I felt really bad about it and never did those things again especially when I hurt my mom and dad.

He grew up in the small town, Homestead, Pennsylvania. The Chief of Police, at the time, befriended the Veze family. The officer was concerned with problems in Chris's family and wanted to do all he could to help. Proving to young Chris that there is more to a police officer's job than meets the eye of the citizen, who only notices them pulling over speeding drivers and patrolling neighborhoods. In fact, most officers go beyond the realms of everyday duties and are active members in their community. They truly care about the citizens of their town. They show compassion to family's hardships and take an interest in helping them when possible. This has become the side of law enforcement that Chris shows to the citizens in his community.

In 1996, Chris graduated from Cornell High School in Coraopolis, Pennsylvania and he achieved his lifelong dream, in 2002, when he graduated from the Police Academy. His first job in law enforcement was with the Stowe Police Department in McKees Rocks, Pennsylvania. He was a patrol officer with them from 2 years. During his last year there he also served with the Neville Island Police Department. He worked several part time positions due to the fact that the majority of police departments in the Pennsylvania area were only hiring part time officers.

The Neville Island PD disbanded in 2006 due to budget problems and from there Chris went on to the Verona Police Department; then to the Tarentum Police Department. While working part time with Tarentum; he also worked full time with the Duquesne University Police Department as a security guard. He then waited patiently for a full-time position to open.

It was not until February 7, 2007, that Chris was offered a full-time position as Patrolman at Bell Acres Borough Police Department in Sewickley, Pennsylvania. He is currently a full time Police Officer at Carlow University located in Pittsburgh

Pennsylvania. Chris carries the same desire, zeal, and compassion for law enforcement when he is off duty, as well as when he is on patrol.

Officers know that dangers can lurk around any corner, literally. For Chris, one of his injuries came while he was on foot patrol and a resident approached him to file a suspicious person report. When she left the yard, she failed to secure her front gate and her dog escaped. It was known for being "very aggressive toward anyone that came near the property." The dog lunged for Chris and left nowhere for him to retreat. He reached for his service weapon but had no time to fire at the animal.

Chris: I took a step back, crouched low to the ground protecting my groin area and punched it in the snout. The dog still got a bite in on my left thigh going through my pants and breaking my skin. The injury was minor. The owner yelled a command at him and it returned to her.

Chris has also learned that many times people want to change their lives for the better but are simply unsure how to do it. Chris once arrested a man on drug and assault charges and while transporting the subject to the jail he confided in Chris about everything he had done wrong in his life. He stressed the relief he had that Chris was the officer who arrested him because of his overwhelming compassion, humility and genuine concern. This was a changing moment for Chris; he saw an opportunity to get to the underlying issue of why the subject chose this lifestyle. It is, in fact, a chosen lifestyle.

Chris, in return, confided in the subject about his life and how God pulled him through his difficult trials. No matter what was going wrong, God was there in Chris's life. They prayed together and by the time they reached the jail the subject's attitude about God and the police had changed. What an amazing opportunity for Chris to change this man's life for the better, as well as, aid him in bringing God into his heart. For Chris, calls like this make the injuries and dangers of the job worth coming to work!

Chris continues to be a positive role model in the lives of teens and young adults and has earned the reputation of a police officer who will go out of his way to not only help people but guide them as well.

Once a teen took the initiative to approach Chris and his twin brother, Brian, (who is also a police officer) to tell them how he wanted to change his life but like so many others, he did not know where to start. The teen had been involved in gang activity and selling drugs.

Chris and Brian's mentoring and guidance helped change the young man's life. He went on to join the United States Army, though unfortunately, he lost his life on the battlefield. That young man paid the ultimate sacrifice as he died a hero for America during his first tour of duty in the War on Terror. Chris will never forget his face or the sacrifice he paid for the rest of us.

Chris: While being a beat Officer I had the opportunity to be a good role model and light in the lives of many teens and young adults struggling with anger, violence, drugs, and gangs. I encouraged them and did the best I could to get them on the right track in life. Being a police officer is more than going to a job every day. It's a life decision to put another person's interests above your own no matter the circumstance. Sacrificing your own safety and well-being is a strength that comes from the Almighty God. The "Police Officer's Prayer" says it all.

*If a teen stated that they wanted to follow in your chosen career path, what would be your advice for them?

Chris: Law enforcement is the best profession in the world! It is very rewarding if you have the compassion and desire in your heart to help and serve others with integrity, professionalism, commitment, dedication, and honesty. If you want to be a Police Officer for the wrong reasons, and there are many out there who make the news often for their actions, don't even think about it. You make us all look bad.

And yes, catching the criminals and keeping them off the streets from harming others feels great!

Charlotte Hopkins

Police Officer's Prayer

Lord, I ask for courage ~
Courage to face and conquer my own fears ...
Courage to take me where others will not go ...
I ask for strength ~
of body to protect others,
and strength of spirit to lead others ...
I ask for dedication ~
Dedication to my job, to do it well,
Dedication to my community, to keep it safe ...
Give me, Lord, concern for those who trust me,
and compassion for those who need me ...
And please, Lord, through it all,
be at my side ...
Author Unknown

Senior Police Officer John Aiton

During Senior Police Officer John Aiton's law enforcement career he has learned that not all rescues have a happy ending but each and every call makes an impact on the officer involved. Much like the call that John responded to that involved four high school teenagers on a quest for illegal alcohol. The boys were at a high school basketball game and left to go to a "bootleg house" to pick up alcohol. Shortly after they left the house, they were in a car accident. Their Volkswagon Beetle went out of control and struck a utility pole on the driver's side.

John: When I arrived, I found "Buddy" draped over the passenger's seat the passenger's door was open and two of the three friends were trapped in the backseat. When I got to "Buddy" he was not breathing. I began rescue breathing on him. I was covered with blood and glass when the ambulance finally, arrived. "Buddy" died that night. While I

142

was trying to save "Buddy" his two friends in the backseat
were yelling and cursing at me to stop and get them out.

The fourth friend was caught by the police, fleeing the scene of the accident. He was not even trying to get help for his friends. He did not care that his friends were trapped and dying. He simply, did not want to get into trouble. John will never forget the sight of this young man leaving his friends to die. John stayed throughout the call to console the parents of "Buddy" when they arrived.

John got a late start in law enforcement; it was not until he was 31 years old when he decided to become a police officer. Before making the leap into the law enforcement world, he went to Seminary School and taught there for three years. John went on to apply for his first position at South Carolina's, Rock Hill Police Department where he is now a Senior Police Officer.

Officer Vince Jeter served as his role model and is described by John as, "the best cop I ever knew!" Throughout his career, John has served as a Patrol Officer, Special Investigator, Detective, D.A.R.E. Officer, Hostage Negotiator and Chaplain. During the first 15 years of his career he worked as a Resource Officer for South Pointe High School.

His wife, Barbi, had the biggest impact on the man he is today. Being a police officer is difficult and loving one can be just as difficult! It takes a strong woman to stand by a police officer. They cannot always be there during family events, holidays and special occasions. These women understand and accept this. This is their sacrifice for their community. When a police officer finds a woman, who stays by his side throughout everything she becomes his rock, just as Barbi is for John.

Since the incident at Columbine High School, students and teachers have learned to work together when there is a threat or a risk of danger. When John worked as a School Resource Officer (SRO) he received a tip from two students that a transfer student was seen on the bus armed with a gun. He boasted that when they arrived at school, he was going to load the gun in the bathroom and pull the fire alarm on his way out. He planned on shooting at students as they emerged from the classrooms.

John: We quickly located the student. We got him out of class. We also found the gun and bullets. Was this just a student running off at the mouth or would he had gone through with it? Background of the student's history, I found out why he was transferred. At his previous school he brought a gun to school and shot the gun in front of that school. This day we avoided a tragedy by students doing the right thing and coming to us with the report.

Several weeks after the incident, MTV came from New York to visit the school and did a story on the events of that afternoon. They stressed that with the students and officers working together that day they saved numerous lives and countless injuries. The turn out that afternoon could have been horrifying. This is why there is such an importance today for School Resource Officers (SRO).

During his first job as an SRO he met a young man named Dylan who came to have a lasting effect on him. One week into the school year, John first noticed Dylan standing about 25 feet from him, just watching John. During days that followed, John would notice Dylan standing behind him, still just watching him. Dylan was a sweet young man. He was born healthy but an accident at the hospital left Dylan mentally handicapped.

John befriended Dylan and they had daily talks about his interests, which mostly evolved around law enforcement and police officers. One day John brought a sergeant's badge that the officers used for safety patrol and pinned it on the army green coat Dylan always wore to school. Dylan wore it with pride and never took it off. As the school year rolled by, Dylan and John became great friends.

John: He would wait in the faculty lot for me to pull in. Dylan was my friend. We would go and patrol the parking lots. I met his parents and they were great and very happy with our

144

friendship. They told me Dylan would go crazy thinking he saw me when they were out riding around town. Our friendship made news, yep the local newspaper came out to see and hear about "Officer Aiton and Dylan."

In our state the special needs kids have to leave school at age 21. So, Dylan graduated with his class. I was there so scared he might panic on the stage. He did great and we were all waiting for him when he came off. I went to his house for a reception after graduation.

After Dylan graduated the two would continue to meet in town. Five years later, John received the news that Dylan fell ill and passed away.

John: I went to my friend's funeral. His mother just broke my heart telling me how much I meant to Dylan. The truth is Dylan did more for me than I ever did for him.

Though John is no longer an SRO he continues to support the students from South Pointe High. He has lost students over the years to accidents, suicides and DUI wrecks. He attends each and every funeral, as well as, each graduation ceremony.

*If a teen stated that they wanted to follow in your chosen career path, what would be your advice for them?

John: I would advise a student to do anything else besides police work, if they could. #1 reason is they could get hurt doing this job and I don't want anyone to get hurt. Police work is a calling and those that have that call can't do anything else. We answer the call and get up strap on the gun and pin on the badge and answer the call. We stand between good and evil every day.

The poem, "Because There is a Hero," was written by Megan Lewis in dedication to Officer John Aiton.

Because there is a Hero

Megan Lewis

I sleep soundly at night, because there is a hero.
I walk safely to school, because there is a hero.
A brave strong hero dressed in blue.
Shield made of brass, fast as a bullet.
Quickest and wisest among people I know.
These heroes are cops.
And before I go to sleep,
I will thank God that we have them.

This article about Sergeant Aiton and Dylan Hughes appeared in the "Charlotte Observer" newspaper.

"ROCK HILL PROFILE DYLAN HUGHES/IN CAHOOTS"

BY Erin Lee Martin/Column: UNORDINARY PEOPLE
Charlotte Observer, February 26, 1997

ROCK HILL - It is sunrise and Dylan Hughes is alone, standing sentry behind Northwestern High School.

Already he has checked the tires on his school bus and waved as the driver rolled back to the street. He has scanned the parking lot for suspicious characters, and carefully adjusted the worn AAA police badge on his jacket.

He is waiting - as he waits every morning - for Sgt. John Aiton, the Rock Hill police officer assigned to the school. Aiton is late, and Dylan, a Northwestern junior with severe mental handicaps, shifts from foot to foot watching the road.

"Sgt. Aiton sleeps in," he announces finally, digging his hands into his pockets. "I have to write him up. I'm getting the evidence on him."

It's a game between friends, a never-ending thriller of cops and criminals played out in snatches between classes and lunchtime snacks. It is also the best reason the shy 19-year-old has to climb on a school bus every day and brave a world that too often pretends he is not there. "It gives Dylan a purpose," says Kelly Gainey, a Northwestern coach whom Dylan threatens to arrest daily for skipping lunch. "Every kid needs something to look forward to when they come to school."

It begins in the gray light of morning. Some days, when Aiton slides his white cruiser into the lot and flashes its blue lights, Dylan jumps foot to foot and whoops like a wookie. If the spotlight plucks his shadow from the morning twilight, he leaps hollering for the closest dark doorway.

Aiton steps from his car and fixes Dylan with the raised eyebrow and pointed finger of a late-night television detective. Between smothered smiles, the tough-guy barbs sound inked into comic strip bubbles.

"I'm watching you," Aiton jokes one recent morning. "I'm getting the evidence, and I'm gonna bring you in." Dylan shoulders his book bag and giggles nervously, "You don't have any evidence," he says," You sleep too long to get any."

Dylan and Aiton have been friends for three years, ever since Aiton caught sight of the teenager circling him in the school cafeteria, staring at his badge. He spent weeks trying to draw Dylan out.

Then he heard that Dylan had bought a police scanner. Aiton asked him about it, and the words tumbled out so fast Dylan had to stop for breath. He thought he heard me on the scanner at night and he would tell me all about what I did, and I just played along," Aiton says.

Soon Aiton invited Dylan to patrol the parking lot with him during lunch. He brought Dylan a list of police radio codes, and then a badge. They hatched plots about catching coaches who skipped lunch or parked in the no-parking zone behind the school.

Suddenly, teachers and students began commenting on the change in Dylan. They noticed the wide eyes and giggles whenever Dylan spotted Aiton across the campus lawn. And for the first time, anyone who wanted to talk to Dylan had something to talk to him about. "He's starting to come out of his shell," says James Blake, an Assistant Principal who passes Dylan in the parking lot each morning.

"He's like a refresher when you get on campus."

Sgt. Aiton got it out of him by becoming his buddy," says David Bartles, a teacher who joshes with Dylan during lunch. "He sparked that one interest, and he keeps it going, and Dylan can't get enough of it."

Follow Dylan for a day, and you'll see a half-dozen students inquire about Aiton's whereabouts or tell Dylan where to find the officer. Dylan starts most conversations relating Aiton's latest antics: how late he came to school, or where he parked his car.

"Sometimes he drives you nuts with it, but at least he's talking," Bartles says.
Dylan lost a sheriff's badge playing in leaves last year and Aiton gave him a silver and green badge that AAA makes for student patrols. His green coat is frayed and torn on the spot on the left breast where Dylan carefully pins and repins his badge. At night it sits on his bedside table. He is terrified of losing it. "I used to be a sheriff, but now I'm a sergeant," he says solemnly.

Dylan's mother, Marybeth Hughes, credits Aiton with playing role model for her son and being patient enough to listen to Dylan and understand his sometimes-garbled speech. His mental handicaps and learning disabilities make it difficult for the teen to interpret the world, and he is frightened of change. He spends most of his day in special-education classes, in a desk huddled at the back of the room near the teacher. His brain fixates on things sometimes, and he repeats himself endlessly.

The friendship with Aiton and the stories he and Dylan create make Dylan braver, says his mother, a teacher in Charlotte. "He doesn't have a lot of friends who share an interest in him and listen, so it means so much to him."

For Aiton, the reward is watching students and teachers stop to chat with Dylan. He notices that Dylan is picked on less often, that fewer of his peers seem intimidated by his handicaps.

"A lot of people, in the beginning, they thought, here's a weird guy. I don't think they think that anymore," Aiton says. "He can contribute a lot if they just spend some time with him."

Dylan will finish at Northwestern in 1998, when he turns 21 and becomes too old to attend public high school. It is a bittersweet date for everyone but Dylan, who shrugs and says he will move into the police station and live with Aiton.

For now though, he will chatter with Aiton and plan criminal crackdowns each day after school until the bus rolls up to take him home. He is always first in line.

He turns to Aiton before stepping aboard. "You're eavesdropping," he tells him. "You're listening. You're getting evidence on me. I'll get you tomorrow."

Lieutenant Darrell Wright

Police Officer Justin Vinson

Police officers first used K-9's on the job in the late 1800's; specifically, for riot control. The German Shepherd was the first breed used by the police. The pitbull was the first dog used by the military police and is also the first dog to be awarded a medal. U.S. Customs uses smaller dogs with more drive and energy. They are often used to run along conveyor belts in the airport to sniff luggage and packages. There are a wide variety of breeds now used by the police. They range from the Belgian Malinois, Labrador Retriever, Dutch Shepherd, Rottweiler, Boxer, Doberman Pinscher, American Pit Bull Terrier and even Japanese Akitas.

The K9's have come a long way. Today they are used for more than crowd control. They sniff out drugs, weapons and bombs, track down missing people, handler protection, search for evidence, assist in search and rescue and track down suspects on the loose.

Two of Tennessee's finest K9 Officers are Darrell Wright of Englewood Police Department and Justin Vinson of the Newport Housing Authority Police Liaison (Project Cop).

Darrell Wright always believed that police officers are born with a deep desire inside of them to protect and serve the public. If you do not have that inside, you then you will be unsuccessful as a cop. As many have said, it is a thankless job; and for that reason, choose a career in law enforcement for the pride of protecting your community and no other reason.

Darrell: It is not a job for everybody, it truly takes a special type of person!!!! My grandparents were my biggest influence because they always taught me to respect anyone in law enforcement. All I can ever remember wanting to be, was a cop!!!

Justin Vinson graduated from Cocke County High School in 1998 and it was three years later when he decided to make law enforcement his career.

Justin: My heroes have always been my dad - who taught me always do right and treat others the way you wanted to be treated. God of course for giving me the heart and compassion to help others. And Superman was always a large influence in life. I actually do my job as to fight for Truth, Justice and the American Way. Andy Griffith - watching the show growing up gave me understanding how to handle people on all aspects no matter their backgrounds or way of life.

In 2004, Justin began working with the Tennessee, Newport Police Department as a Patrolman. He has since taken on the position of Department Chaplain and in July 2006 was appointed the Newport Housing Authority Police Liaison (Project Cop).

In February 2008, he picked up his K9 partner, a Belgium Malinois K9 (a Shepherd breed) named, "Halo." His position of K9 cop has not taken away from his duties as Project Cop. In fact, Halo helps on special assignments with the

Housing Authority, as well as, routine street narcotic enforcement. But it was working with children that was his greatest motivator.

Justin: No calls stand out more than the ones where you go in and find a child hurt, abused or abandoned. Each time a child is put in a situation like that you just want to beat the head in of the person that put that child in that situation. Any call involving a child in danger will always touch me more than a standard call from day to day.

Justin has taken his work a step further and has become a member of the group "501" where he holds the title of "Sith Lord." His feels his greatest satisfaction is "doing charity work and putting smiles on many kids faces!!!"

The group, 501, is a charity group that dresses up as Star Wars villains and participates in charities to raise money for sick and dying children. They also visit Children's Hospitals and Children's Group Homes. They volunteer for groups, such as, Toys for Tots, Make a Wish Foundation, Cancer Society and any children's charity that wishes to have them.

It was shortly after Darrell first became a police officer that he made the move from Jacksonville, Florida to Tennessee at the request of his now ex-wife who felt that Jacksonville was too dangerous a place for police officers. Once in Tennessee, he was a Reserve Officer in Athens and moved on to McMinn County Sheriff's Office. His final transfer was in 1999 to the Englewood Police Department. In 2005 he was made Chief of Police at the Englewood PD.

It is at Englewood PD that he was trained as a K-9 Officer. He and his new partner, Riley, (a German Shepherd), first traveled to Denver, Colorado for their training. On completion they travelled to Indiana to the Von Liche Kennels; to earn their certification.

At the Von Liche Kennels there are five – six classes offered every year and up to 100 teams trained during that time. There is a five-week course in the training of narcotics and explosives. During their patrol course, officers are taught grooming and health, first aid, leash control, vehicle bail outs and gunfire scenarios.

Some of the most rewarding moments in Darrell's career are when those he arrested for drugs later thanked him and explained that it was his arrest that was their wake-up call to stop abusing drugs and straighten out their lives. Darryl's chief goal as an officer is to remove drugs from the street.

Darrell: I am not crazy enough to think we will get everyone off of drugs & wipe them out, but as long as we can still make a difference we need to continue the fight!

Darrel and Justin both had their share of experiencing the rough side of being a police officer. While Darrell was making a DUI arrest, the driver attempted to flee the scene with Darrell hanging off the side of the vehicle. After he brought the car to a stop; the fight continued outside the vehicle. During the scuffle, he was struck on his left hand by an asp (collapsible baton) carried by a fellow officer. Fortunately, his hand was not broken but it was stiff and sore for several days following.

Justin had the misfortune of falling victim to a careless driver refusing to yield so he can do his job. He was directing traffic struck and was struck by a Chevy pickup truck that was hauling a trailer. The vehicle struck him on his right side which caused him to flip over the trailer and land onto a 4-lane highway. He suffered from a pulled muscle in his right ankle but did not let that slow him down; he was back to work a week later.

*If a teen stated that they wanted to follow in your chosen career path, what would be your advice for them?

Darrell: If any teenager is considering getting into law enforcement I would have them check with the local police departments & see if they have a reserve or explorer program. That sometimes is a good way to get your foot in the door.

I would also tell them they need to stay in school, stay away from drugs & trouble & study hard, stay in shape & be 100 % dedicated to the job and stay focused on your goals!!!! I would also tell them check with the local police departments & see if they have a reserve or explorer program. That sometimes is a good way to get your foot in the door.

Justin: I am an ordained minister and youth minister. One of my youth is actually following my footsteps. He is enrolled in criminal justice class in college and going to the police academy in Spring 2009. He plans on attempting to be hired by the Newport Police Dept. soon afterwards. So, my advice is get a taste of what the job actually is, by riding reserve or having others in the family being an officer and giving advice. Put make sure it is what you want to do in life. There are good times and bad times, but you will make a difference.

"The Working Dog" is a tribute to our 4-legged heroes!

The Working Dog

My eyes are your eyes,
to watch and protect you and yours.
My ears are your ears,
to hear and detect evil minds in the dark.
My nose is your nose,
to scent the invader of your domain.
And so you may live,
my life is also yours.

Deputy First Class James A. Jones, Jr.

The first time Deputy First Class James Jones responded to an assistance call, was when his sergeant and a fellow officer were conducting an eviction and the man refused to leave the property. The bank had foreclosed on the home and sent movers to haul everything away. The resident protested and refused to leave.

Though Jim was several miles away he was the closest backup available for the officers. While they waited for Jim's arrival the sergeant and deputy peered through the living room to see the man hiding behind the sofa acting like a nervous groundhog, popping his head from behind several times.

When Jim arrived, the three officers approached the front door as the Sergeant shouted out to the man of their arrival and that they were entering the home. He knocked on a thick oak door and when he did it swung open. They found they man lying face down on the living room floor. He had a 410-gage shotgun across the lower part of his body. He had committed suicide by sitting on the floor, using a wooden dowel through the trigger guard and using his feet to push the trigger.

Jim: We could still smell the cordite from the gunpowder in the air and watched as his heart was pumping the blood through the wound in his head.   He was going to have a "suicide by cop" by pointing his shotgun at us, but instead of seeing two Sheriffs, he saw three, and at the last minute, decided that was the time to do it. He had been planning this for some time. He left a suicide note, which contained a copy of the eviction notice. In it, it explained his plans, and he left Post It notes on all objects in the home to show which person he wanted them to go to. He placed a manila envelope with the remaining monies he had left and the keys to all locks and doors throughout the house.

Jim was in kindergarten when he started playing with police cars and police toys. He still holds treasured photos of him as a little boy with his toy cop cars. It was always an interest to him and as he grew it became his destiny.

There were several events that paved the way to his career in law enforcement. It began when his friends in the police department would take him on ride-alongs. There was also the time when Jim was honored to have F.B.I. Director

J. Edgar Hoover deputize him to assist on a manhunt for a cop killer from 1947. He got the final push that he needed when a State Trooper told his father that he wished Jim was wearing a police uniform like his. Four years later, he was graduating from the police academy and earned the position of Deputy Sheriff.

Jim: It was hard work for six months through the academy where we were run to death, exercised both mentally, and physically to exhaustion, and lost sleep at nights to arrive at that day. Although my dad has been gone since 2004, I feel he is still with me, acting as my guardian angel while I am on patrol.

His father was an oak of a man and would become Jim's greatest role model. He was a World War II Veteran and a survivor of the Great Depression.

As an officer, Jim has served on the Fugitive Warrant Squad and the Field Operations Section, where he was responsible for warrants in the civil, juvenile, and criminal sector. He was responsible for seizures of private property, evictions, foreclosures and garnishment of wages. He also served summons and subpoenas.

Serving warrants has proven to be a dangerous aspect of police work. No one wants to be served and some will fight to the death to stop it.

Bullet proof vests are a must when serving a warrant but there is not much in armor that can protect a cop from dogs. Jim learned that lesson when he was bitten by a man's large Boxer dog. During another call, Jim and several officers were serving a warrant on a man who resisted arrest when a scuffle broke out and Jim ended up on the bottom of a pile up; there were three officers on top of him.

One of his more bizarre calls came when attempting to serve an arrest for a child support warrant. They had been tracking the subject's whereabouts and traced his steps to his mother's house. She allowed the officers entry into the home, so they could ask her a few questions. She informed them she had not seen her son in a while. She was a widow and lived alone. His partner asked if he could search her home to satisfy the warrant. Again, she agreed and while his partner looked upstairs; Jim went to look in the basement.

She had been in the basement throughout the day; washing laundry. Observation is a key point of his job. Jim noticed that there were men's shirts and pants neatly folded in the clothes basket. If she truly lived alone then why were there men's clothes in the laundry? He leaned over the dryer and peeked into her large capacity washing machine. There were two men's work shirts being washed and he felt the dryer moving even though it was not on.

Armed with his ASP baton he opened the dryer door to find the man hiding inside. He was 6'2" and managed to squeeze into the dryer. His hands were folded on top of his head. Jim pulled his service weapon out and held him at gunpoint as he ordered him out of the dryer. The subject was double jointed, and Jim could hear every joint pop. He learned that it is not wise to use sarcasm on the police.

Jim: I called my partner down and got the subject handcuffed. The subject stated he could get out of the handcuffs, and he did. He just worked them loose and handed them to us. Well we got the flexcuffs, and hogtied him, and laid him across the backseat for transport to the Sheriff's Office.

Jim had many days when he worked himself exhausted to get out all of the warrants and find the Wanted people in his community. He can only sleep more soundly at night when he knows that the people in his community can sleep soundly first. In 1996 he went to work for the Baltimore County Sheriff's Office and remains there today for the Field Operations Bureau, Area 8A.

When he is not on duty, he has several interests including bowling and wiffle ball. He has his own guitar building/rebuilding business, named the "Sevenpointe Lutherie." He first opened the business in 1991 and has a deep satisfaction at looking upon one of his own creations. He builds custom guitars, basses, and mandolins. His favorite is constructing cigar box guitars!

Jim is also the founder and Chief Investigator for the

paranormal group the "Paranormal Research and Investigation Society of Maryland" (PRISMd).

Jim: We Hunt the Haunt!! Ghost Chasers are in it for the fad. Ghost Hunters are in it for a hobby. But Paranormal Investigators are in it because it's a PASSION.

One of his expeditions as a Paranormal Investigator aired on the A&E channel.

*If a teen stated that they wanted to follow in your chosen career path, what would be your advice for them?

Jim: My advice is to follow your dreams. Never accept anyone's criticism that tells you that you can't become anything your heart desires. Keep plugging away and overcome and adapt to any challenges before you. If you wish to enter the field of law enforcement, you have to have a "special fire in the belly," to want to help others, and your community.

Remember, that when you enter law enforcement, you are held to a higher standard. Although the field is stressful, it is also rewarding. When you can help your fellow human, it is more rewarding than any award given on paper. And never forget where you come from. That is the most important trait to have.

Deputy Sheriff Bryan Ward

There have not been many dull moments in Bryan Ward's years as a police officer. He has made over 2,000 arrests and has been in 100 high speed pursuits. He has fought countless drug dealers and addicts; chasing them through houses, woods, fields and down public sidewalks.

One of his vehicle pursuits happened in a county that was no more than 575 miles in distance. It was early in the morning and he was the only officer on duty. He recognized the man as a recovering heroin addict that had previously done time for shooting at a police officer in Baltimore. Bryan, himself, arrested the man a year earlier on a DUI. He knew that the man did not have a driver's license but there he was behind the wheel of a car. He was driving reckless, passing cars at 100 MPH and risking a catastrophe as he continued to try to evade Bryan's patrol car.

He radioed for back-up and as the race pursued into the following county and back into his own town he remained on the phone with dispatch. All the while he kept them informed of his whereabouts, so his back-up can locate him. The pursuit came to an abrupt stop on a farm road that he was unfamiliar with. The car chase took him on so many twists and turns he was certain that if back-up was on its way his directions would be useless.

The road was a dead end between several poultry houses and house trailers. The man pulled the car to a stop and began blowing his car horn. As Bryan jumped out of his police cruiser the subject also bailed out of his SUV. Bryan ordered him to hit the ground. The subject looked at Bryan, began laughing, and shouted, "Fuck you!" At that time, several rough looking characters came out of the trailers. Bryan knew he was just led into the wake of a dangerous position. He also realized that the driver was under the influence of drugs.

Bryan: I started to think I was in real trouble. I trained my pistol on him and repeated my command. Not knowing what alliances, he may have had with the persons coming out of the house trailers I had to divide my attention and occasionally train my pistol on them; ordering them back into their dwellings. The suspect declined to get on the ground and, instead, taunted me and then he reached inside the open window to his SUV. I was afraid he would come out with a weapon or that one of the other persons now outside would present a threat or weapon.

Bryan ran towards him and kicked him away from the SUV. He was intending on knocking the suspect to the ground, but the man grabbed the side mirror to keep his balance. He then turned around and charged Bryan, who was now running backwards, attempting to holster his pistol and retrieve his pepper spray. He successfully reached the pepper spray but when he attempted to spray the suspect the wind blew most of it back in his own face.

Once again, the subject ran back to the SUV to retrieve an object through the open window; which Bryan would later learn was a large dagger. Bryan's eyes were swollen shut and burning from the pepper spray. He became frantic, knowing he was outnumbered and was now unable to see the whereabouts of everyone. Even worse, he still did not know their intentions.

He knew that the suspect was determined to get an object from the SUV. He also knew that at this point he was justified to shoot him because he had no intentions of complying with his commands. Bryan chose not to shoot him. He holstered his weapon and once again charged him and this time he brought him to the ground.

Bryan: I have no idea what happened next. I lost all sense of time, sound and reality.

Bryan wrestled with him in an effort to secure him with handcuffs, all the while never knowing how many, IF any of the onlookers were approaching him or if they were going to assist Bryan or the suspect.

Bryan never knew help was on the way and never heard or saw the lights and sirens from another officer who managed to find his way from the sketchy directions Bryan had given over the radio. After several minutes of wrestling with the suspect and striking him repeatedly a familiar voice pulled Bryan off saying "he's had enough."

Bryan: I had not gotten the handcuffs on the suspect but had beaten him into submission. Had help not arrived, I can only guess the number of ways this ending could have gone. The suspect was hospitalized, and I struggled to summarize in detail what had occurred. I went home after completing my paperwork; To this day most of what happened when I tackled him is only a guess.

Expect the unexpected, was a lesson Brian learned during a routine patrol. He drove past a bar just as a call came across the radio of a "man with a shotgun" in that same bar. As he pulled up to the bar, he heard shots from inside. He radioed for back-up and ran towards the back of the building; as a crowd ran out of the bar and hollered to Bryan that the shooter was inside and that he had hostages. He was securing the perimeter when back-up arrived.

At that point, he ran across the front of the building and as he glanced at the open front door, he noticed the man inside had his shotgun pointed directly at him. Until Bryan was able to reach cover, the suspect followed him as if he was zoned in on a flying bird. The stand-off lasted several hours, fortunately, no one was injured in the end. The suspect used mental illness as his defense; was convicted on lesser charges.

Bryan is a 1983 graduate of High Points High School in Beltsville, Maryland. He went to college for carpentry; following in his father's footsteps. The work was financially rewarding but physically draining. At 24 years old he decided to seek a new line of work. It was then that he came across a newspaper ad for law enforcement workers. He answered the ad right away and scored at the top of his class when he took the Civil Service Test.

He accepted his first law enforcement position with the Hardy County Sheriff's Office. He worked there for 18 months, which included four months at the Police Academy. While working with Hardy County, Bryan also worked closely with the Town of Moorefield Police.

The Moorefield Police Chief was impressed with his work in law enforcement and offered him a steady position. At the time, Bryan was newly married and trying to start a family on an income of $14,000 a year. The position in Moorefield included an increase in pay.

Since supporting his family has always been his number one priority; he accepted the offer and resigned from the sheriff's office. The following day, he began his work as a patrolman with Moorefield.

In 1995 while Bryan was investigating a string of arson fires; the trail led to a number of volunteer firefighters. At the time, he had only one friend who worked as a firefighter and it was that "friend" who became his prime suspect. The subject was later convicted and sent to prison. While working alongside the firefighters he grew to have great respect for the work they did. He was so taken by their actions that he joined the fire department as a volunteer and in the first year he was named "firefighter of the year."

He is always thinking of others first and this was the case when Moorefield Police offered to promote him from "Patrolman 1st Class" to "Lieutenant." He respectfully declined the offer. Though he served with Moorefield for 13 years; he was also employed at the fire department, so his family was financially secure with two incomes. He stressed to the Captain that his concern was that other officers, who relied on one income may build animosity towards him. He asked that one of the others be offered the promotion. The Captain understood, and he retained his position of "Patrolman 1st Class."

While on duty he often came across citizens who were sick or injured but only knowing how to administer basic first aid he was often limited with only the ability to comfort the victim while waiting for the ambulance to arrive. This always left him feeling helpless. He has never been the type of man who wanted to stand back and "wait" for help; preferring instead to jump right in and give it his all. This desire is what drove Bryan to make his third career move; to become a paramedic.

During EMT training he felt the desire to learn hands-on as well as in the classroom and he began volunteering as an EMT for a volunteer rescue squad. Bryan didn't intend on becoming a paramedic for a living; he simply wanted to be a better volunteer. Shortly after he earned his EMT-P certification, a friend informed him that the fire department in Cumberland, Maryland was hiring firefighters and paramedics. He went down to take the tests and was hired by the fire department in August 1999.

His schedule at the fire department was 24 hours on and had 48 hours off. There were also vacation days and Kelly Days. The term "Kelly Days" was coined by former Chicago Mayor, Edward Joseph Kelly He requested that city council give firefighters a paid day off after 14 days of work.

Due to his work schedule at the fire department he considered resigning from law enforcement and solely working as a firefighter/paramedic. His police chief asked him to reconsider his decision and promised to work around his fire department's schedule. Bryan was not sure if he would be able to manage both careers but eventually found it to just be "very busy."

He's had his fair share of trips to the emergency room from injuries suffered in the line of duty from both of his jobs. As a police officer he suffered from sprained ankles, twisted knees, cuts & bruises. These occurred during foot pursuits and scuffles from subjects resisting arrest.

As a firefighter he suffered from smoke inhalation and minor burns. He has also twisted muscles in his ankles, knees and his back during these fire calls, as well. He once sprained his back when he fell down a flight of stairs responding to an EMS call. He has been experiencing back strains from lifting patients on EMS calls.

An EMS call that made one of the biggest impacts on him came when he was on duty as a patrol officer and he responded to "a fall." When he arrived at the home, he was greeted at the door by three children, ages 3, 5 & 7. They looked at Bryan and simply told him that their mommy had fallen. He and his partner followed the oldest child to the basement where their mother was doing laundry. She was lying, unconscious, on the floor. She was not breathing, and her heart stopped beating. He determined that her heart was in ventricular fibrillation and lubed up the paddles on the cardiac monitor to commence a series of shocks.

They began their routine safety chants "I'm clear - you're clear - everybody's clear" before each shock. This is a safety measure to make sure no one is touching the patient during shocks. The paddles release a strong current of electricity through the patient's body to start the heart. The shock can seriously injure or kill a bystander.

When Bryan was interrupted by one of the kids tugging on his trousers and asking, "Is mommy going to be ok," he delivered the next set of shocks with tears in his eyes. Though the ambulance arrived shortly after, all of their efforts to save her fell short and she did not make it. At the end of his shift, Bryan went home with a lump in his throat that he could not seem to shake.

Throughout his career, he experienced dozens of calls that made him want to hug his daughter tightly when he gets home. Most of the time, it is from the sight of an elderly patient laying there with no breath or circulating blood. Sometimes though, it is from seeing the life cut short from a young man or woman, or even a child. Blood and guts have no effect on Bryan and most medics do well to look past the unpleasant sights. It is when he has to turn off the sights and sounds of the living that he struggles with his emotions; knowing that they are watching in horror as EMT's do their best to restore life.

Bryan: TV doctors always seem to say it so well to the family members when they've lost a loved one. I've yet to find a painless way to tell the living "there's nothing more we can do for him/her" without feeling guilt; despite following protocols perfectly.

In 2005, the Hardy County Sheriff approached him about a new position in his office. They wanted to put a uniformed deputy in the schools. He told Bryan that he knew a deputy's salary is pathetic, but he would make it possible for Bryan to continue to work his schedule around the fire department's. He was happy to jump ship; back to the sheriff's office. There would not be a vast difference in his duties. He still puts on that uniform every day, drives patrol in his police cruiser and chases bad guys. However, his primary focus now was working with students at Hardy County's five schools.

Bryan remembered being terrified of the police when he was a child and now that he was an officer himself, he can relate to children who were afraid of him. He understood their fears and knew how to ease their concerns. Since he had stood on both sides of the fence between citizens and police officers, he also understood why some police officers seem to be uncaring and standoffish.

Bryan: Indeed, most of the men and women are wonderful and mean well. Sadly though, after a few years on the job; being lied to constantly, seeing only the dishonest, the cruel, and all of the failings of the "justice system," cops get calloused and mistrusting. A thousand "good deeds" and many personal sacrifices are wiped away with a single controversial call. Cops aren't always victims of this exposure. Some begin their careers with the wrong attitude; from day-one, sprouting up a foot taller and gaining fifty lbs each time he or she pins on their badge. No matter how the cops arrive at callous though, the perceptions of the public remain.

When he began his position as a School Resource Officer, he found his first challenge did not come from the children but from his fellow officers and the perception they have about today's teens. He continues to work on bridging the gap between cops and teenagers and defusing the *us against them* mentality. At times he finds himself lecturing more to other cops than he does to the kids. So far, his work has been rewarding.

After years of chasing down criminals he enjoyed changing gears and focusing on other matters. Especially, insuring that students of Hardy County have the best chance at chasing their dreams and avoiding the path of a criminal life, or other destructive behavior.

*If a teen stated that they wanted to follow in your chosen career path, what would be your advice for

them?

Bryan: If a teen asked me about the rewards of working in public safety, I would have to respond by saying "I can't imagine doing anything else." There are emotional consequences to helping people. I'm so proud to be part of this group of loving men and women. We do our best to lean on one another when then emotions run high. Most often, we find a way to clear our thoughts and continue to the next call. Burn-out thought, is not uncommon.

Sergeant Ty Hamilton

The driving force behind Sergeant Ty Hamilton's choice in becoming a police officer was to make a difference in people's lives. His first job in law enforcement was at the Honolulu International Airport where he would have a defining moment in his career and his ability to help change people for the better! He was doing a routine check of a female truck driver's vehicle. She pulled into their scale house and while Ty was checking her paperwork, he noticed discrepancies with her story. Her shipping papers noted that she was carrying 18 washing machines but only 14 of the boxes were full. They were Maytag boxes, but the washing machines were old used laundromat style machines. Old machines would not have to be boxed.

Ty grew more suspicious when the driver began acting nervous. Police are skilled at reading people and he knew that she was hiding something. Ty asked her if she had any children and she told him of her one-year old son and two-year-old granddaughter. He then picked up two pipes and asked how it feels to look at him through those bars because that's how she is going to see her children in the future. She hung her head in shame and admitted to Ty that she was on her way to load the truck with marijuana.

Ty: She became a confidential informant and worked a huge drug case for us. At the end of the case she came up to me and said thank you, "Because of you I can see and be with my children and you pulled me out of a life of crime. If not for you, I would be in jail with the rest of the organization."

He achieved his goal...he was making a difference, the first of many more to come. His next move in law enforcement was with the White Sands Police Department where he served as a Training Instructor, DARE Instructor and a Patrol Officer. He is now a Sergeant with the New Mexico Department of Public Safety and Motor Transportation Division. In 2002 he was appointed the department's K9 Officer.

As I stressed, each and every call can quickly turn into a dangerous situation for a police officer and even a call for an abandoned vehicle can be tricky. There are several scenarios that can fold out in front of the police when they arrive at the scene. It could be a set up for an ambush. It could be a weary driver who pulled to the side of the road to get some sleep. It could be someone injured and in distress or it could be a car that broke down and the driver got a ride. It is the not knowing that leaves police on their toes.

During one of Ty's calls for a possible abandoned vehicle, he followed protocol and went into caution mode as he arrived on the scene. His red flag went up immediately when he found the car with the hazard lights on, keys in the ignition and no one around.

He scoped the area around the car but was unable to find anyone in sight. He rummaged through the contents of the car, hoping to find something that would give him information on the driver; possibly even a phone number to call. Luck would have it, he found the driver's registration, as well as a phone book. He searched through the numbers and was able to find someone with the same last name as the driver.

As he made the call, the voice on the other end of the line, was the daughter of the vehicle owner. She explained to Ty that the owner of the car was her father (a man in his late

70's) and that he was on his way to move in with her. He was taking medication and hallucinated from time to time. She was worried he may have started hallucinating again and wandered off.

Ty retrieved his K9 from his police cruiser and began a search patrol on foot. His K9 immediately picked up the man's scent and led Ty on a path about 20 feet the car, straight towards the missing driver. Ty found the man hiding under the overpass. He was cold, scared and confused. Ty escorted him back to his car and together they contacted his daughter. She was filled with such happiness and relief that she was sobbing into the phone.

Ty: She informed me that her husband was going to fly out to pick her dad up in the morning. She was so overjoyed and stated that words can't express how thankful she was that I found her dad. Those two incidents made me feel so good, especially to know that I had an effect on someone's life that was so positive and just the word "thank you" was enough.

Ty grew up in Hawaii and graduated from Radford High School. As a true Hawaiian, he will always call Honolulu his home. When he was 18 years old, he got into legal trouble over a stolen car and almost went to jail. That scared him straight. To keep himself from getting into further trouble he joined the Air National Guard and went through their Police Academy.

He was interested in law enforcement long before then. He always enjoyed the TV programs C.H.I.P.s, SWAT and Hill Street Blues. His interest in law enforcement went beyond the TV screen and into the streets of his own community. He admired the work of the police in his town; the actions they faced and the difference they made in people's lives. Each day that Ty puts on that uniform he continues to reflect the actions of those officers.

*If a teen stated that they wanted to follow in your chosen career path, what would be your advice for them?

Ty: Stay in school, get an education, go to college and stay out of trouble. But I always put emphasis on the school part.

Police Officer Dave Busch

When Officer Dave Busch set out to become a police officer in 1973, he could not have imagined that he would one day be traveling to Africa to train new recruits in the war-torn country. He began his career as a Police Explorer and when he turned 21, he was hired to serve as a Police Officer for the Los Angeles Police Department. His next move was to the Cooke County Sheriff's Office in Gainesville, Texas, where he was an Investigator and Patrol Deputy. Today he is with the Community Safety Institute in California.

In 2007, Dave was one of a 5-man team from America chosen to serve as an Emergency Response Unit Instructor in Liberia, Africa. He was excited to take what he learned in law enforcement through education, training and street smarts and educate the Police Academy students in Africa. They are a torn country emerging from a Civil War and rebuilding as a democracy.

The team from America was accompanied by several instructors from other countries as well, such as Turkey, Germany, Philippines, Serbia and the Czech Republic. They spent 18 months in Liberia training a 500-member Emergency Response Unit in conjunction with the "United Nations Mission in Liberia." The Unit would become equivalent to our SWAT Team in the United States.

He was surprised by the country's extreme lack of educational and defense supplies and had to learn quickly how to improvise on much needed materials. Firearms training proved most difficult. He used hand-carved guns to teach team movement and numerous other skills associated with tactical movement. Most recruits did not have experience with guns. The weapons they were used to carrying were called "cutlass" better known as "machetes."

Dave: Every day was a new day to learn how to make the most out of what we had to work with.

His first SWAT class was given to the Liberian National Police in January 2008. Sessions were three months long and during that time, Dave and fellow recruiters stayed in rundown buildings with tin roofs. Classes were held in tents. They didn't have electricity or drinking water except in the main compound and there was a lack of food.

Dave: They also treat the water, it doesn't taste great because the amounts of chlorine or other chemicals used but it's safe to shower and brush your teeth, we mostly use bottled water for drinking and cooking.

On a lighter side, Dave and the recruits also found themselves in a dispute with a monkey that was camped out in a tree that was nestled against their dorm. The monkey often enjoyed flinging objects at their tin roof...at all hours!

Some of the tactics he educated the officers in, included responding to riots, hostage rescue, domestic terrorism and high-risk warrant service. Dave was also in charge of teaching tactical first aid, high risk vehicle and bus take downs, building entry, hostage rescue and shooting drills.

He taught recruits how to properly handle the American made M-4 A-3 rifles along with close combat pistol training. His list of duties continued on to educating the officers on map reading, close combat skills, close protection training, crowd control and emergency police operations.

His experience in Africa was rewarding as he watched a team grow from "having tactical experience" to a well-disciplined group of tactical officers. He was also involved with building the gap between the military and police so that they can work together and rid the animosity between the two groups.

Dave: The void must be filled by highly motivated and trained individuals whom want their country to work and never be thrown into civil war again as they saw for 14 years. A professional democratic police agency is one of many steps how this country is being turned around.

*If a teen stated that they wanted to follow in your chosen career path, what would be your advice for them?

Dave: From the start pursue your dreams. Do everything you can do even before you actually start your career such as the police explorer program for example if you wanted to be a police officer. Always look at the many ways or things you can do to help you focus on what you really want. Every profession has sub professions/skills which you should also look at doing. Being a police officer requires you to be in good shape, a good writer, and a good people person. Each of those is separate skills that can be worked on before ever becoming a police officer. All careers have them so seek them out and start early developing the sub skills of your chosen career.

Sheriff Karl Dailey

Sergeant Cheri Saunders

"Suicide by Cop" is when a person wants to die but does not want to kill themselves, so they attack the police in an attempt to get the officer to kill them. Sheriff Karl Dailey experienced this and was forced to shoot and kill the perpetrator. He was not proud of what happened that day and has never forgotten the events from that afternoon. The victim's family later told Karl, that he was a career criminal and wanted to die. His family knew it was eventually going to come to that point. He had gotten into legal trouble and was going to go back to prison; instead he chose "suicide by cop."

Karl was worried how the public would react, but no one seemed to notice. It may be because the man was Caucasian. Had he been any another race, Karl may have been chastised by the media.

Karl: Most people that criticize the police don't know what they are taking about. Cops have to have eyes in back of their head and learn to trust their sixth sense. Among the police, it's a love/hate relationship. We fight like hell among ourselves, but we will die for each other. We abuse each other horribly in jest but we don't let anyone else do it.

Sheriff Karl Dailey and Sergeant Cheri Saunders are two of Nebraska's finest Police Officers. When Karl graduated from high school in 1972 the United States was in the midst of a military draft; recruiting young men to fight in the Vietnam War. His 18th birthday was fast approaching. Karl was given a high number and was not sure if he would be drafted. He was in a quandary of what path to take. He did not support the war, but he also did not support the stance that the protesters stood.

Karl: I didn't want to be a part of the protesters because 90% of what they spewed was garbage and I was tired of hippies complaining about the world.

Though he was not a part of the war protest he was indeed a political buff. The voting age had just been lowered to the age of 18 so he was able to cast his first vote for president and has never missed a vote since. His first vote was for Richard Nixon. He was always impressed by the character traits and beliefs of Harry Truman and Ulysses S. Paton. He liked Paton's attitude of "if you are going to do something; do it right, don't screw around" and he has lived his life with those same attributes.

At the time, his other options were to go to work or enroll in college. He jokes that he would have preferred anything other than going to work. He considered college and at the time, universities were introducing the Criminal Justice program. Karl was already walking that fine line between making something of his life and heading down the wrong road. Fortunately, for Karl, he had several State Cops and a Detective around who saw something good in him. They stayed on him and watched after him and his activities. It was those officers who influenced Karl to make law enforcement his chosen career path.

He had a variety of other positive role models in his life. His parents were his biggest influences. As a native New Yorker (Long Island) his other influences were Roger Maris, Mickey Mantle, Yogi Berra and "any other Yankee baseball player." He was an avid reader, particularly comic books. He liked the honesty, integrity and morality of Sergeant Rocky, Superman and Batman.

In 1976 he left New York to start a new life in Nebraska. It was there that he got his start in law enforcement working for the Chadron Nebraska Police Department. In 1986 he successfully ran for Sheriff of Dawes County. He took office in 1987 and continues to hold the position of Sheriff.

In all of his years of law enforcement his worst injuries have been a black eye and a knot on the head. He believes that keeping himself safe has been from a combination of luck and staying smart. He feels that most officers develop what he calls the "John Wayne attitude." They can be over zealous and react too soon. He believes cops need to temper that desire with intelligence and common sense. In some situations, the injured police officer can become part of the problem.

For many years, police were taught to "wait until there are two of you before you go into a situation." This is old school thinking now. After the incident of Columbine, they have changed that strategy.

With Officer Saunders, her interest in law enforcement began in middle school. She was hooked on tv shows, such as, Charlie's Angles, Police Woman and any other series that was cop related. Her father was a police officer and she admired the work that he did.

Cheri: I loved the fellowship/brotherhood the officers had with one another. All his co-workers were like fathers to me.

In 1993 she became a Nebraska Certified Officer and her first job in law enforcement was with the jail. From there she moved on to Court House Security and Civil Process; where she spent five years. She was then transferred to Investigations and was recently promoted to Sergeant. For 10 years she has been a Defensive Tactics and Spontaneous Knife Defense Instructor for her department.

She is an expert on performing forensic interviews on children who have been a witness to or became a victim of violent crimes. Her greatest satisfaction comes in putting a child's "bad guy" in jail. Her first forensic interview was with a little girl that survived an attempted sexual assault at the hands of her father. The young girl has since been adopted by her foster parents and is a now happy well-adjusted child.

Karl and Cheri have since joined the ranks of police serving in the, "Kids Come First" group. "Kids Come First" is a group started by Gene and Barbara Black; to protect children from predators on the Internet. Their focus: Teaching children how to avoid becoming victims of online predators and who to contact if they are approached.

Karl: Protecting children from predators on the Internet is an absolute must. I'm an "old dog" trying to learn new tricks, I have wonderful and dedicated teachers to help me and nurse me along. I'll do anything I can to assist "Kids Come First" and any other child protection organization working in this area. I'm glad to be aboard and looking forward to working with you all.

Children are vulnerable to predators because of their innocent and trusting nature. They need adults like Karl and Cheri to stand between them and the danger of online predators. To the children, they are the *nurse* to their physical injuries, the *therapist* to their mental scars; the *mentor* for their questions on life; and the *teacher* educating them on ways to be safe online. Most importantly, they are the *friend* that children need and can always go to. They also provide the youth with the much-needed education to move from "victim" to "survivor."

"The Ocean and the Internet" is a piece that Cheri feels describes what it is like for children online.

The Ocean and the Internet

Picture This:

You are swimming in the ocean. You know that it is filled with sharks and sharks are predators. You can't see them but, you know they are there. You don't know what direction they will come from or if and when they will attack.

The Comparison:

The Internet is just like the ocean. It is filled with strangers and strangers may be predators. You can't see them; their monitor is their mask. You don't know who they are; they can be anybody they want to be, and you don't know what their intentions are.

Like sharks swimming in the ocean searching for their prey; online predators surf the net searching for their next victim. They can be someone down the street or someone across the country. Like the shark an online predator will travel miles to get to their prey.

*If a teen stated that they wanted to follow in your chosen career path, what would be your advice for them?

Karl: I've told my two sons, "don't do it." I don't like the direction law enforcement is going today. A long time ago when cops first started, we were part of the community. We looked after, protected and cared for our community. Now it's "us the cops and everyone else." Today people want to kill us and hurt us. New cops aren't involved in the community anymore. We were all once members of church, we assisted in boy scouts little league, to be a part of the community. Now most cops don't want to live in the community that they patrol.

They don't serve on boards and aren't involved in the community. They have the "us and them attitude." Make sure the community is important. Don't just protect and serve, be a part of the community. We need more cops to replace the us and them knuckleheads.

Cheri: You have to want to "help people" in this job. You cannot get in it for the money. Typically law enforcement is a low paying job. Stay in school, study hard, stay in shape and find peace with Our Father in Heaven. I seriously believe you cannot be successful in this career or maintain a healthy mental status without a strong belief in your religion.

Internet Acronyms Every Parent Needs to Know:

POS - Parent Over Shoulder
PIR - Parent In Room
P911 - Parent Alert
PAW - Parents Are Watching
PAL - Parents Are Listening
ASL - Age/Sex/Location

MorF - Male or Female
SorG - Straight or Gay
LMIRL - Let's Meet In Real Life
KPC - Keeping Parents Clueless

TDTM - Talk Dirty To Me
IWSN - I Want Sex Now

NIFOC - Nude In Front Of Computer
GYPO - Get Your Pants Off
ADR - Address
WYCM - Will You Call Me?
KFY - Kiss For You
MOOS - Member(s) Of the Opposite Sex

MOSS or MOTSS - Member(s) Of The Same Sex
NALOPKT - Not A Lot Of People Know That
2NITE - Tonight
AEAP - As Early As Possible
ALAP - As Late As Possible
AWGTHTGTTA - Are We Going To Have To Go Through
This Again

B4YKI - Before You Know It
BOHICA - Bend Over Here It Comes Again
BRB - Be Right Back
BRT - Be Right There
CWYL - Chat With You Later
C-P - Sleepy

CYT or SYT - See You Tomorrow
E123 - Easy as 1, 2, 3
EM? - Excuse Me?
EOD - End Of Day
F2F - Face To Face
FOAF - Friend Of A Friend

HAK - Hugs And Kisses
ILU or ILY - I Love You
IMNSHO - In My Not So Humble Opinion
J/C - Just Checking
KOTL - Kiss On The Lips
L8R - Later

LD - Long Distance
LMK - Let Me Know
LOL - Laugh Out Loud
NAZ - Name, Address, Zip
N-A-Y-L - In A While
NM - Never Mind or Nothing Much
OLL - Online Love
OSIF - Oh Sh** I Forgot
OTP - On The Phone
QT - Cutie
RN - Right Now
ROTFL - Rolling on the Floor Laughing

RU - Are You...?
RUMORF - Are You Male Or Female
SITD - Still In The Dark
SMIM - Send Me an Instant Message
SMEM - Send Me an E-Mail
SO - Significant Other

SOHF - Sense of Humor Failure
SWDYT - So What Do You Think?
TOM - Tomorrow
TS - Tough Sh**
TTFN - Ta-ta for Now
U-R - You Are..?

WFM - Works For Me
WTH - What the Heck
WUF - Where Are You From?
WYRN - What's Your Real Name

Police Officer/Rescue Diver Benjamin Quick

Lesson One from day one was, *NOTHING IS EVER WHAT IT SEEMS!* Officer Benjamin Quick's first job as a

Police Officer was in a small town of about 800 people and on one of his earliest calls, he was answering a "domestic in progress." He was the only officer on duty at his department; though county officers were in route to assist him. As Benjamin approached the door, he said that it sounded like all hell was breaking loose. At that moment a flash of adrenaline rushed through him as he played out scenarios in his mind of what might be happening on the other side of that closed door.

He peered through the windows to gain a concept of what was happening so he can determine how to approach the situation. He couldn't get a good view but heard the children screaming, "Don't hurt me daddy!" At that moment his backup arrived. As he approached the front door he could see a Christmas Tree waving back and forth in a violent manner. He proceeded to pound on the door. The mother answered and allowed the officers to enter.

Benjamin: As we spoke to the mother who was putting together the tree, the dad walked out of the bedroom. He was being held back by his three children, one was hanging off his neck like a monkey, one was wrapped around his stomach in a manner of trying to climb up his body and the last one was wrapped around his leg and sitting on his foot in order to be carried. It was a very comical sight to see. It taught me the VERY VALUABLE LESSON that NOTHING IS EVER WHAT IT SEEMS.

What Benjamin feared was a violent call, with the possibility of abuse, turned out to be a dad clowning with his children while their mom attempted to assemble their Christmas Tree.

Lesson Two came some time later; that was: *FOLLOW YOUR INSTINCTS!* If it feels wrong; if it feels dangerous; then it probably is. He was answering a call for a man attempting suicide, Benjamin approached the house with caution; using his light as a cover. As he crossed the front of the home, a man opened the door and invited him inside.

Benjamin: I was asked by a male in a real freaky voice, "What are you doing?" Just in his tone my gut sank and my body went on high alert. It is crazy how you will process information. I went on such an alert I could hear the crickets chirping 3 blocks away.

The man continued to try and persuade Benjamin to come inside to talk to him but Benjamin refused. As he stood in the doorway, Benjamin noticed he was holding something in his right hand but he refused to reveal what it was and the view was blocked by the door.

As SWAT officers arrived, they made their way into the home and found the man trying to fix his shotgun. The weapon jammed after he fired it the first time. He was quickly taken into custody and that night he was placed in a mental hospital. It was during the interview between the man and his psychiatrist that Benjamin would find out how close he came to lose his life that night.

Benjamin: He told the interviewer about that officer who showed up last night (me) and if he would have "came in when I asked him," I was going to force him to shoot me or I was going to kill him. From that point on I have followed and never second guessed my gut instinct.

Growing up, Benjamin often thought of a career in law enforcement and after the 911 attacks he decided it was time to make that move. He is now a patrol officer with the Charleston Police Department and serves as a Rescue Diver on their Dive Rescue/Recovery Team.

Throughout his career he has held several positions, including:

M-16/AR-10 Armorer
ASP - Tactical Baton Instructor
ASP - Tactical Handcuff Instructor

PPCT - Defensive Tactics Instructor
PPCT - Spontaneous Knife Defense Instructor

It was in the 1970's when law enforcement started to utilize scuba diving as a way for police officers to perform underwater search and rescues, recovery and investigations. When Benjamin Quick got his first taste of "Underwater Rescue" he wanted nothing more than to join that rank of Police Divers!

Diving hasn't just become a part of Benjamin's job; it's his passion. He has since launched, Policediver.net, a business of apparel for dive and rescue workers and scuba diving enthusiasts. Much of his apparel is custom designed for divers, teams, police and firefighters as well. All items are of the highest quality, since he knows firsthand, that on the job...second best is not good enough! He also offers numerous different designs.

*If a teen stated that they wanted to follow in your chosen career path, what would be your advice for them?

Benjamin: I would say: Take some form of martial arts like Aikido and not Taekwondo. Study hard and workout harder. The criminals are in jail working out and plotting ways to harm us, so we have to be in shape and ready for them. Law enforcement is full of demands and takes toil on your personal life. Once you become a cop people change and friends that you thought were close you will become distant. There are thee b's that will kill a career in law enforcement and watch out for them and they are Beer, Boobs, and Bills.

Lieutenant Joseph (Joe) Laramie

It was a few days before Christmas, in the early 1990's, and Lieutenant Joe Laramie was just sitting down to have lunch at the annual City Christmas Luncheon when a call for an "unresponsive person" came over the radio. The victim was only 45 years old and he was found by his wife. She left early in the morning to run errands and left him to sleep because she did not want to disturb him. She did not realize that he died sometime during the night.

Joe: I spent the next 1.5 hours sitting in the kitchen of this home with the wife, talking about anything and everything I could think of to help her through this tragic event. The Christmas tree was right behind me, with presents bearing his name. They had an 18 yr old daughter who was Christmas shopping and I prayed she wouldn't come home while her father was still in the house, or especially while they were taking him from the home. She didn't come home while I was there. Every Christmas I think of this very nice woman and wonder what her life is like now. It was one of the hardest situations I have ever been in, yet I find it one of the most rewarding.

His compassion for the public and keeping them safe was the motivator for Joe to become a police officer. When he was a high school senior, he weighed his options on what to do next in his life but was uncertain which road to take. All he knew for sure was he did not want a desk job. At the time, he was friends with several police officers who gave Joe his first taste of police work and he liked what he saw. He saw the value in the work they did and the symbolism of what they represented.

In October 1974, he went to work as a part-time police dispatcher with Missouri's Glendale Police Department. He took on the dispatch position full time in April 1976 and three years later he was assigned his first position as a police officer. He remains with the Glendale PD today.

Early in his career as a patrol officer, he was also assigned the position of the Department's Juvenile Officer. His first case involved a new family in the neighborhood, who had a 15-year-old "problem child." The teen was continuously landing in trouble at home, as well as, school and was now repeatedly running away. After several conversations with the family it became increasingly apparent that there were significant underlying issues causing the girl's reckless behavior. He continued to delve into their mounting problems until he was able to pinpoint exactly where things started to go wrong for their daughter.

Joe learned the reason the family moved from their previous residence was because the teen became pregnant and had given her baby up for adoption. The parents were ashamed of the daughter's actions and had trouble dealing with the facts of the situation. They wanted to move where no one would be aware of the circumstances their daughter was involved in; a fresh start for everyone involved. Well, that is how they saw it anyway.

That was it! The root of her problems stemmed from the day she gave her baby away. She was not able to talk about the events with anyone because in her home; it was a closed subject. As Joe grew to know the young girl, his chief concern was to get her to stop running away from home. She bonded with Joe and confided all of her problems and feelings to him during their many talks.

He tried to convince her parents the importance of setting her down and apologizing for the way they handled her pregnancy and the adoption. They eventually took his advice and did apologize to her; but by then it was too late! The parents had taken too long to react to the hurt they caused their daughter. The day after their talk, she ran away once more and never returned.

Joe: Her parents found her a couple years later living in another state and doing very well. She taught me so much about dealing with kids and family dynamics. My wife of more than 20 years was treated much the same way as this teenager. She became pregnant in high school and was sent away to live with another family and gave her daughter up for adoption. I have to say her story ended very well. In 2001 her daughter contacted us and is now as much a part of our family as our other children.

A teen pregnancy should be handled delicately. If an adoption is needed be sure the teen receives counseling before and after it happens; even if she appears to be handling things strongly. The physical and emotional scars left on a woman from such an event will come out in one form or another if they are not dealt with from the start.

Joe was shown by the teens that he counseled the importance of compassion, understanding and communication during rocky times. Sometimes being a hero is more than throwing your body in front of a victim. A hero is also the officer who serves as the rock and the support for teens. As compassionate as he can be, Joe also knows how to rule with an iron fist when the moment calls for it.

*If a teen stated that they wanted to follow in your chosen career path, what would be your advice for them?

Joe: I would tell him or her how rewarding it is to work for a community. I would also add how hard it is on your family. The working hours can be physically demanding, and working holidays is difficult on your family. I was asked once however, if I considered my career successful and rewarding, and if I did, why wouldn't it be recommended to others. That said, I would tell a teen that if I had to do it all over again, of course I would.

Charlotte Hopkins

The Hero in the Night

Next time a cop stops you because you are driving too fast,
Remember he saved you from that day being your last.

When you think he's picking on someone,
Why not think of what they could have done?
Next time you call him a name,
Would he have called you the same?

How would you feel to see a child beaten black and blue?
And knowing there is not much you can really do.
You can arrest them and hope they stay in jail,
But, too many times it doesn't work that well.

To see the face of someone right before they die,
When he can't, but all he wants to do is cry.
To break up a fight, knowing later it will be worse,
And from his help, all that came was him being cursed.

To know that people don't respect what he chose to do,
But day after day, he's out there to protect people like you.
To see drugs sold to a child younger than his own,
Makes his heart ache and long for his home.

The job has no glamour, doesn't even pay well,
He does it because he cares for more than himself.
He cares for you and he cares for me,
He's out there hoping we will all see.

He took a path not many would take,
And he chose it for our sake.
He's a remarkable soul, a Hero in the Night,
When all is well, he's not in sight.

But, if you ever need him, he'll be right there,
Not just because he's a cop but because he cares.

Police Officer Travis A. Stoffer

The fact that any call can swiftly move from routine...to emergency...to life-or-death is what keeps the police, like Officer Travis Stoffer, on their guard at all times! This all too surreal moment happened for Travis when he responded to a vehicle accident late one night. Travis had just finished getting gas for his squad car when the call came in for a vehicle accident on the other side of his town. As he radioed that he was responding to the accident; they informed him that the vehicle was now on fire.

When he arrived, he saw that the driver was still trapped inside the car. It was a winter night and the roads were slick. The driver lost control of the car and hit a tree head on. There were three citizens already on the scene. They were trying to pull the driver from the car and put out the fire that was now creeping closer to the man inside, but the flames were unbearable. When Travis approached the vehicle, the man was moaning and crying out, "Help me!"

They tried desperately to rescue the man from the vehicle. Just as the flames reached the driver, they were able to extinguish the flames. They tried to pull him from the twisted metal that surrounded and trapped him inside. Meanwhile, his moans soon turned to gurgles. They were unsuccessful in their attempts to rescue him and he died trapped in the car.

Travis later learned that the man was unconscious when his vehicle hit the tree but woke upon impact. His feet were tucked under the seat and became entrapped. The fire caused the console to melt across his lap. When they put out the flames with the fire extinguisher the console hardened around his legs which is why they couldn't pull him out of the car. There was not anything that Travis could have done differently to save the driver.

Among all of the of car accidents Travis responded to; the youngest victim was 18 years old. The young man just worked a double shift and fell asleep at the wheel. His car wrecked into a sign for a tire company; causing the car's motor to crash through the front of the vehicle and lodge into his chest. The dashboard that was pressed against him was holding the motor in place. The pressure was keeping the young man alive. When they lifted the motor off of him, he passed away.

The teen victim was a recent graduate and had his whole life ahead of him. It broke Travis's heart to see him die in that manner. Travis may not have been able to save him, but he was there for his last few moments of life. The young man did not die alone and that in itself is a blessing. The last words he heard were compassion from a police officer who wanted his last few moments to be in peace.

Travis knew when he graduated from high school that he wanted to go into the police academy. As a teen he came to know Jefferson Hills Police Officers, Chris Gallis, Jack Fullmer and Bob Welsh He admired their attitudes and the work they did for the community. Mostly, he applauded their dedication and how good they felt about doing their jobs.

Travis: They are a good group of guys and they made it look like something that I wanted to do.

Travis worked at Lucianno's Pizza in Bethel Park for a year to save up enough money to attend the Police Academy full time. He got his jump into law enforcement in 1993 with the Elizabeth Borough Police Department and his career started down a long road from there.

He served Elizabeth Borough for five years and was then transferred to the Glassport Police Department. During his two years with Glassport, he simultaneously served with the Lincoln Boro Police Department.

His next transfer found him at the McKeesport Police Department and within two years he was transferred once more to the Clairton Police Department. While at Clairton he also worked with the Forward Township Police Department.

An incident early in his career; that he refers to as one of his more "ironic moments" happened when he was a patrol officer for the Elizabeth Boro Police Department. He was on duty when a call came out for a shooting at a local bar. The victim was a man who Travis arrested numerous times in the past. Because of that, the victim hated Travis, as the officer puts it, "he hated the ground I walked on."

The man was shot twice in the chest and there was no way to save him. When Travis arrived, he cleared back the crowd and held the man in his arms. Moments later he passed away. The last thing he saw before he died was that the police officer, who he hated more than anything, was comforting him in the last moments of his life. It does not matter what names you call the police or how much you claim to hate them; when you need them, they will always be there for you, no matter who you are or how you treat them.

Injuries have become par for the course for Travis while he is on duty and he jokes that "Aflac hated him" when he worked at the Clairton Police Department, due to the many bruises, cuts and pulled muscles he suffered while on duty. It's a rough neighborhood and the police work hard and tirelessly to protect the citizens there.

It was no laughing matter though when he suffered his worst injury to date. It happened when a tri-axle, that was deliberately driving in the wrong lane, crashed into the side of his patrol car. The driver was swerving around traffic trying to get through the other cars quickly, all the while, trying to make a left-hand turn. Travis, in his patrol vehicle, was pulling out of a parking lot to answer a call. While other drivers veered to the side of the road for Travis, the trucker was only thinking of reaching his destination and plowed into him; destroying the side of his car.

His injuries from the accident were extensive. He continues to suffer from herniated discs in his back, permanent hearing damage and bone spurs on his neck and left shoulder. Bone spurs are bumping that push on the nerves and cause muscle spasms. They have caused Travis to lose all feeling in his left knee, at times he loses feeling in his left arm and he cannot sit in one position for an extended time. He has since been diagnosed with PTSD, particularly since it occurred while he was on duty.

Today Travis continues to serve the Floreffe police department and while on duty he often assists West Elizabeth, a neighboring community. West Elizabeth is a small town with a small police department. One way he helps is by doing patrols and keeping a watchful eye; making sure all are safe. Never wanting to leave anyone waiting for help, he tries to serve where he can. This was never more evident than when a call for help came from a young girl who ran away from her home in the night.

The teen was in an altercation with her step father and was afraid to go home. She was fairly new to Pennsylvania; having lived there for about two years. She was isolated from the community and only knew a few people. She felt extremely alone in the small town.

There was one person that she knew for certain she could go to. It was to her house that she went that night. When Travis overheard Elizabeth Borough receive the call about a teen in need of help, he raced to assist her.

She confided into Travis all that had been happening in her home and he put his best effort forward to get the help she needed. Before he left that night, he gave the young girl his business card. He wanted her to feel safe in knowing that he was a phone call away and she could call if she ever needed him.

The young girl stayed with the neighbor for a brief period and is now living back at home. He always wondered if he did enough for her that night. What Travis does not realize is that he helped in more ways than he realizes. That young girl still carries that business card with her every day. She no longer feels scared and alone because she knows that she is in fact, not alone. When a child is in danger the worst feeling in the world is that empty feeling of having no one to turn to. She is more relaxed and at peace now that she knows that she does have someone looking out for her and he is a phone call away.

*If a teen stated that they wanted to follow in your chosen career path, what would be your advice for

them?

Travis: Anymore if I didn't know the person then I would advise against it. You have to be dedicated and you have to be a strong individual to do it right. And you have to want to do it for the right reason. You have to want to do it for the community or you won't succeed because you have everything working against you today. The politics of it will disgust you to no end. There are a lot more rules and paperwork than before. It is a very backwards system. It is very frustrating when you want to give the victims their justice and you know they aren't going to receive it. The job is best suited for people with good common sense. So, I would only advise it if I know the person and I know they are dedicated and have good common sense. You have to relate to many different types of individuals. You have to have good morals; they are extremely important. There are so many people out there that want to hurt us. You have to have good communication and reaction.

Learning to Trust the Police

There are often times when people tend to be bitter and unrelenting towards the police. The police know that in some cases it is because those same people had a negative encounter at some point in their life with law enforcement. Things like that leave a bruise inside that causes pain or even anger during any connection with the law in the future. It is not the fault of the officer or the people at hand. One bad experience can scar someone for life against the very people who are there to protect them. Breaking down that wall of fear and mistrust is the hard part.

My early experiences with the police are heartbreaking and, at times, I felt they were unforgivable. I watched the police turn their backs on me when I needed them the most. I was a child and I relied on their protection. They let me down and befriended my attackers. I grew up believing that no officer of the law could ever be trusted. Until one day as an adult, life taught me a hard lesson.

It was then that Jefferson Hills Police Officer Shawn Revis would teach me to trust the police. He showed me that not all police officers were like the ones who turned their backs on me. Most officers actually do their best to protect their community because they have the desire and drive to "protect and serve."

My nightmare began when I was nine years old. It was then that my parents were divorced. I went to live with my father and I had a new "step mother." Her family of bikers were evil and extremely abusive and showed me a side of life that I had only seen in movies.

There were times when the police would show up at their biker parties for which I thought was to break up the violent and illegal activities. It was usually the same two officers. To my surprise, they were there to converse with the bikers. It was like these people were friends with the police. How can that be? There were drug sales, drug abuse and drug activities going on right in front of them. I thought, "Why aren't they doing anything?"

It is not how I thought police officers acted. These officers witnessed drug activities and abuse and stood by silently. In school they would talk to us about safety and urge us to go to the police if we were ever in danger. I just shook my head in disbelief. I knew that you really cannot go to the police for help.

The mayor was one of the friendliest people in our town. He welcomed the children in the neighborhood to stop in anytime to sit and talk or just say "HI." I enjoyed my visits to the mayor and when I saw the light on in his office I popped in for a visit. Even if he was busy talking to the officers, he would invite children in to grab some candy from the jar on his desk.

Once when I was there, I had a black eye and a fat lip from a beating that my father gave me, and the mayor asked what happened. I wanted to tell him, but I could not. I heard conversations about what they would do to the mayor if he ever found out *what was going on* and that they would *make sure he didn't talk*. I did not want to be the one to get the mayor hurt. I told him that I was swinging high on the playground swing set and that I jumped off and landed wrong.

My final breach of trust happened one evening when another fight broke out at my house. Among the people in the fight were my father, "step mother," bikers and even their wives/girlfriends. It was one big brawl! During the fight, I was hit a few times by my father. To get away from the fight, I ran over the hillside and ran right through the front door of someone's home.

I did not know who's home it was, so I knew my family would not find me there either. I ran in and shouted, "I need help." There was a family in the living room watching TV. When I ran in, they jumped up and immediately took me in their arms. They asked what was wrong, but I was crying so much that I could not talk.

They told me to sit on the stairs and they will hide me. They said that no one will hurt me there. As I sat on the stairs, I heard their conversation in the living room. One of the men was saying "who is she" and "what is going on?"

The woman, who I now recognized as my school crossing guard, said "Don't ask her any questions right now, she's scared, if she wants us to know what is going on; she will tell us." Inside I was screaming for help, but I "knew" there was no help out there for me.

While I sat on the step, she checked on me and brought me a glass of cold water. Within fifteen minutes I heard a knock on the door. One of the women said, "The police are here, they will help her." Moments later, an officer walked to the stairs and reached for my hand. I had never seen him before, so I thought just maybe this one will help me. I trusted him and went with him.

When I was put in the back of their car, I thought I was finally going to get help. I was beaten, swollen and shaking. One officer looked back at me and said, "We can't take her back yet, we have to ask her what happened." The officer driving the car replied, "She's fine, aren't you fine, tell him you are OK." The second officer replied, "Clearly she's not OK, somebody's been hitting her." The driver became irritated and said, "Look don't ask questions OK, our job is to take her back home." He smiled at the other officer and said, "Just don't look at her." The second officer gave me a sad smile and turned around in his seat, never looking back again.

I thought then and there that I was going to die in this town. I knew that no one was ever going to help me. As I laid down on the backseat, I told myself that I would never trust another police officer as long as I lived. I hated them all. They could have helped me and chose not to.

At 13 years old, I ran away from my father's house and went to live with my mother. I took with me the lesson I learned about the police - they cannot be trusted! I told myself, do not talk to them, do not confide in them and if you ever need help - they will not be there!

Through the years, I was never friendly towards any police officer. I called them names and was abusive with my words. When they attempted to be friendly towards me, I shunned them away. I would never even say "hello" to an officer that walked by me. In fact, just being inches away for a police officer made me boil over insde with anger and hatred. An officer once asked me "Why I act like I hate them?" I told him that "it's not an act, and that I do hate them" and since I do not know which of them are dirty cops, I just see them all as dirty cops.

When I learned that my sister was dating a police officer, I instantly felt that I just did not want to know him anymore. When I saw him in that navy-blue uniform, I flashed on those officers in the car that night and I felt sick to my stomach. After that just being around him made me nervous and tense.

When I was 17 years old, I was having problems with our local mailman who developed a crush on me. He wrote me letters, sent me gifts and photographs and when I received letters from someone I was dating in the army; he delivered them...ripped in half. Shortly, after that, he started calling me on the phone. I contacted the postmaster for help. He started an investigation and when he saw that everything, I said was true, even he urged me to go to the police. I refused to do it. I told myself long ago that I would never again go to the police for help and I meant it.

It was not until two years later when he finally left me alone, only because I moved to a new town to get away from him. But I never went to the police. I believed that they would not help me.

I never pushed my bias opinions about the police off onto others. When I taught preschool, we gave a lesson to the children about police officers. Despite my coarse feelings toward the police, I never spoke ill of them to my students.

I felt that was not fair to the children. I also thought it was morally wrong to instill negative values in them, such as, not trusting the police. I told them that the police were their friends and that they could trust them.

Part of me wondered if there was a police officer who would not ignore a child's cry for help. I also taught the children to go to the police if they were ever being hurt. However, I always added that if the police do not help them then they can go to a church, their teachers or even the firemen. I told them to just keep "telling" until SOMEONE helps them. In my personal life, I still had no trust or respect for the police.

It was not until I was 33 years old that I would learn just how wrong I was about the police. It was on a night when I was at home, sitting in my living room watching tv. It was a warm night out, so I had my door open. Since I live in a small safe community, I did not feel threatened. I heard a knock on my door and when I realized that it was almost midnight my first thought was that, "someone must need help," so I answered the door. That was a mistake!

The man at my door was drunk and tried to make his way into my house. When I would not let him in, he pulled me outside and attacked me. I was never going to let myself be a victim again, so I fought back. I fought with everything I had inside of me and was able to get away and run back into the house.

I was crying and scared and I called my sister for help. She told me to call the police...again I flashed back on the two officers in the car that night. I said, "They aren't going to help me." She said, in a sarcastic tone,"Of course they are going to help," and then she yelled at me to call the police. This time I did! I hung up and called 911 emergency.

Within minutes the operator was telling me that the police were outside. She said they were not sure which house was mine and they need me to come outside or turn on my porch light. I walked onto the porch and there were several police cars outside. When they came in the first officer, I talked to was Officer Shawn Revis. There were several officers in my house and more walking around outside.

For the first time my cry for help was being answered. Officer Revis was as kind and gentle as any man I have known. He talked to me and listened while I cried. He never looked away. I was embarrassed, but he acted in such a professional manner that he made me feel relaxed. When the officers left, he came back sometime later to see how I was and to let me know what he and his officers were doing.

When we had the preliminary hearing at the magistrate's office, I was nervous but still thought that I would be fine, until the police showed up with my attacker in handcuffs. A sense of fear rushed through me and I said I could not go through with it and ran out of the office.

I was sitting at a table outside when Officer Revis came and sat down to talk to me. He never talked down to me or treated me with the "victim mentality," he just talked to me in a comforting and friendly manner. He always knew what to say and how to act to make me feel calm and sure of myself.

He explained my options about whether to testify or not. He also said his only concern was that I was OK. He went on to say that he was on my side and the decision to testify was mine. The DA had other ideas. He wanted to pursue the charges.

I just wanted to go home, hide under my covers and never come out. I guess I was not as brave as I always thought I was. The only way that I was going into that courtroom was if Officer Revis was there with me. He was the only person I felt safe with at the time. I could not believe it myself; this "police officer" was the only person that made me feel safe.

At each hearing, his presence gave me strength; something I never expected from a police officer. Several months went by from the magistrate's hearing and the day of our trial in Pittsburgh.

During that time, I lived in fear. I would not answer my door whether it was 11:00 in the morning or 11:00 at night. I kept my window blinds down when I went into the kitchen and hardly ever turned on the light. Sometimes I would even cook dinner and wash dishes with only the living room light shining in to guide me.

As the weeks turned to months my disdain and lack of trust for the police began to chip away. Officer Revis always assured me that I was safe and that he was there if I ever needed any help. His reassurance got me through this tough time. He once told me that the night he got the call to come to my house he was on the other side of the neighboring town, but he still made it to my house in two minutes flat so not to hesitate to call for assistance.

He explained every court procedure to me. He always let me know what all of my options were and what to expect from the hearings. He never lied to me or mislead me about anything. I found that to be comforting and respectful! This officer was compassionate and professional, he showed me a new side of what police officers are all about. He is a credit to his uniform, his department and his community.

I thought of how I previously acted towards the police, how unfair I was to them. I wish I could go back and apologize. I wish I could explain to them that it was not anything that they did, it was all me. How terrible I must have made them feel with my rude comments and calling them dirty cops.

I lost my faith in the police long ago and it was not just or right, but it was something that I could not help. I failed to give the police the respect that they honestly deserved because I let those two officers, from that night long ago, convince me that they were all bad. I cannot be the only one who responded to the police that way or for that reason. If only the police knew why some citizens feel this way. It is not that we hate them, it is that we are afraid to trust them.

My small town is now protected by a new Police Department, but I will always remember Officer Revis. I will never forget the "human side" that he showed me from behind the badge! He taught me about the life and death risks that they take...without hesitation, just to protect their community.

Now I am always friendly to the police when I see them. There have been times when I became upset with the police officers for what someone else did but I always apologized shortly after for my actions. I will chalk that up to my Irish temper! Thanks to Officer Revis, I knew that the police did not deserve that treatment. They do deserve our support!

I am grateful to Officer Revis for what he did for me and for what he taught me. I will never be able to show him enough how much his attention, kindness, professionalism and consideration taught me about what the police truly are like. That little girl who said she would never trust the police grew up to find a hero in Officer Shawn Revis.

Now when others disrespect or belittle police officers, I jump to defend them. We should not criticize these men and women who risk their lives to protect us! They should be commended and thanked for what they do for us. Like those who walk up to a soldier, shake their hand and say, "Thank you for all that you do," that is what we should do for the police, even just once.

Today's officers put up with verbal abuse, take on violent criminals and at times work themselves exhausted. Yet, they still come to work every day with a smile on their face and one agenda on their mind - protect their community. So, let me be among the first to say to law enforcement everywhere - "Stay safe, keep up the good work and thank you for all that you do!"

Section II

Fallen Heroes

A Cop on the Take

First, he takes the oath.
Now look at all he takes -

He takes it in stride when people call him pig.
He takes time to stop and talk to children.
He takes your verbal abuse while giving you a ticket you really deserve.

He takes on creeps you would be afraid to even look at.
He takes time away from his family to keep you safe.
He takes your injured children to the hospital.
He takes the graveyard shift without complaint because it's his turn.

He takes his life into his hands daily.
He takes you home when your car breaks down.
He takes time to explain why both your headlights have to work.

He takes the job no one wants - telling you a loved one died.
He takes criminals to jail.
He takes in sights that would make you cry.
Sometimes he cries too, but He takes it anyway because someone has to.

If he is lucky, He takes retirement.

He takes memories to bed each night that you couldn't bear for even one day.

Sometimes, He Takes a bullet.

And, yes, occasionally he may take a free cup of coffee.
Then one day he pays for all he has taken, and God takes him.

From the earliest days in law enforcement, there have been police officers that put their best foot forward to instill law and order and keep their communities safe. Like any other profession they have their bad apples but unlike those other professions...if one police officer does something wrong, they all have to pay, across the country. Their job is one of the most dangerous, yet they get the least amount of credit or respect. However, they are not in it for the applause or pats on the back. They do it because they have a drive, an instinct, so to speak, that simply tells them they need to be out there. They want to protect the people of their community. It is that simple! Any officer will tell you; once you hold this drive inside of you, it stays with you forever.

A more disappointing aspect of their job is that their biggest danger is "people." The ones they swear to protect will be the ones who will murder them in cold blood. Some out of anger and still others will murder a police officer because they think it will keep them from going to jail. In reality, it will just extend their jail time. When they stab a knife into a police officer's neck or shoot a bullet into their head, they are not seeing that this is more than just a police officer in front of them. That "cop" is someone's child, someone's spouse, someone's best friend, someone's parent, someone's sibling, someone's aunt/uncle or even someone's grandparent! That "cop" is a person with hobbies and dreams of a future. But their killers do not think about that; all they see...is an obstacle!

Mike Pratt, father of fallen officer, Jason "Tye" Pratt, of Omaha Nebraska, said it best when he described "why" the police are heroes.

Mike Pratt: Do you know why police are heroes? Because they are willing to put their lives between you and danger; and they don't even know you!

In the early 1800's, years would go by without a police officer being killed in the line of duty but today a month does not go by without an officer being murdered. From 1812-1815, no police officers were killed on duty. Also, from 1819-

1821, there were no deaths of police officers.

The punishment for killing police officers once varied on whether you were a man or a woman. On August 4, 1823, Constable Elijah Chenault was killed by a woman who he was sent to to retrieve property from because she did not pay the debt she owed for the item. She struck Constable Chenault on the head with a stick that caused a fatal wound. In that time period women received more lenient sentences and Constable Chenault's assailant was sentenced to a year in prison and received an $85 fine. President James Monroe later dismissed her fine after she served her year. Constable Chenault served with the Alexandria Police Department in Virginia.

The times have changed but the dangers for law enforcement are just as real. The police once chased horse thieves and now chase car thieves. The most common weapons used against them were once hammers and pistols and now they are assault rifles and knives.

Even serving warrants has always been a deadly job for law enforcement. On September 9, 1816, Sheriff Caleb Hewitt, of the Davidson County Sheriff's Office in Tennessee, was struck in the head with an ax when serving a writ. This was 6 months after he was elected sheriff.

On October 9, 1818, Deputy Sheriff William Huddleston attempted to serve papers and collect a fine. The resident of the home beat him to death with a wooden stake. He then buried the deputy in a shallow grave and escaped to Canada with Sheriff Huddleston's horse. He was captured and returned to the United States. Deputy Sheriff Huddleston served with the Schoharie County Sheriff's Department in New York.

Watchman Lewis Leuba, of the New York City Watch, was among 12 officers sent with warrants to arrest five men on April 10, 1836. The assailants resisted and became combative. While Watchman Leuba fought with one of the men, another came behind him and stabbed him in the back with a "dirk." This is a dagger with a blade attached. Three days later, he died from his wounds.

On November 24, 1845, while attempting to serve a warrant, Constable John Horton was stabbed several times and had his throat slit. The warrant was still in his pocket when officers found him. Constable Horton served with the Augusta Police Department in Kentucky.

Constables are dedicated to getting their criminal, no matter what. On December 2, 1853, Constable James Quinn, of the Chicago Police Department, approached a notorious hideout known as "The Sands" to serve a warrant. As he was walking the prisoner back to the jail; the subject asked if he could return to the Sands to retrieve his property. When they walked back in, the owner attacked Constable Quinn; breaking one of his ribs and injuring his jaw. During the assault, his prisoner was able to escape.

The next night, Constable Quinn returned to the Sands with a new warrant for his escaped prisoner and was once again attacked by the owner. That assault resulted in more broken ribs and a punctured lung. Dedicated to getting the job done and bring the assailant in on his warrant he went back to the Sands a third time. This time he was armed with a second warrant for the owner of the establishment that attacked him. He was successful in arresting both men. However, his injuries worsened and the following day he died from congestion of the brain.

Constable Jerry McCrory was shot and killed on December 15,1980 while serving a misdemeanor warrant. Constable McCrory was just approaching the house and was ten feet from the door when the door flung open and the subject inside fired on him with a 12-gage shotgun; shooting him in the chest. Constable McCrory served with the Rankin County Sheriff's Department in Mississippi.

There was once a time when the New York Police were not allowed to carry guns. This rule was amended after the death of Patrolman George Dill on January 10, 1865. Patrolman Dill served with the Buffalo Police Department. He and his partner were on a routine foot patrol when they heard a woman's cries of "watch" and "murder." It was approximately 2:00 AM and the woman was awakened by a prowler. The officers ran to her home. As they approached the house the prowler shot at them. Patrolman Dill was shot in the head and died at the scene.

Dangers on the highway are cautions they have become all too familiar with. Today as law enforcement directs traffic the dangers are just as real as in the mid 1800's when law enforcement directed pioneers across the rivers.

On April 29, 1853, Deputy Sheriff Rodney Badger was helping a family with six children cross Utah's Weber River and their wagon overturned. Deputy Badger immediately dove in to rescue the mother and her children. He was able to rescue the mother and four of the children. When he went back for the last two children he was overwhelmed by exhaustion and the cold and he drowned. Deputy Badger served with the Salt Lake County's Sheriff's Office. His body was recovered a year after the incident.

Trooper James Savage of the Connecticut State Police is one example of an officer killed by a careless driver. On January 22, 1986 he was making a traffic stop when a car in another lane drifted into his path and struck and killed the trooper. He served the Connecticut State Police for 18 years.

On October 22, 2006, Deputy Sheriff Margena Silvia Nunez also fell victim to reckless drivers while trying to control traffic. She served with the Lee County Sheriff's Office in Florida. She was directing traffic at the scene of a previous fatal accident when she was hit by a drunk driver.

The weather has taken quite a toll on law enforcement during their long hours of street patrol and outdoor duties. On July 13, 1870, Patrolman John Regan died of sun stroke after walking his beat for seven hours in extreme temperatures in Memphis Tennessee.

In Nevada, (Deputy) Undersheriff J.J. Ellis died from the cold temperatures while he was collecting court fees. He served with the Elko County Sheriff's Office. When he failed to return; a massive manhunt searched for Ellis, but they were unsuccessful. Two months later several hunters found the body of Undersheriff Ellis. The fees he collected that day were found with his body along with his record book. The date of his death is recorded as March 21,1874.

Also, in Nevada, on March 24, 1998, Officer Russell Lee Peterson was killed during a Search and Rescue practice session when a block of ice fell on his head. The 6-man team was climbing a 160-foot frozen water wall when the ice began to break off. Officer Peterson held tightly to the rescue rope to keep his partner safely against the wall to avoid being hit by falling ice. When they pulled his body from the fallen debris; he was still holding on to the rope that saved his partner's life. Officer Peterson served with the Las Vegas Metropolitan Police Department.

On September 14, 2004, Park Ranger Suzanne Roberts was struck by a boulder while she was clearing rocks after a landslide at the Haleakala National Park in Maui, Hawaii. She was clearing debris from the road when a boulder fell from the cliff and struck her in the back of the head. She died at the scene. Witnesses used her radio to call for help.

January 18, 1898 is the first recorded death of a Bike Cop. Patrolman Frederick Lincoln of the New York City Police Department had just aided the motorman of a streetcar but accidentally omitted information from his report. He was trying to catch up to the street car when he struck a pedestrian. Patrolman Lincoln was thrown over the handlebars and his head struck the corner of the curb.

On April 20, 1899, Patrolman Thomas Meagher was the first police officer to be killed from being struck by a vehicle. Patrolman Meagher had just helped two women to cross Broadway Street and found himself stuck between north and south -bound traffic. A vehicle traveling south struck his right arm; knocking him down. He was almost run over when a private citizen noticed him and helped him to his feet. He then helped Patrolman Meagher walk to the Hudson Street Hospital. His arm was broken in two places between his shoulder and elbow. He died several days later on April 27, 1899, from complications to his injuries. He also served with the New York City Police Department.

On November 10, 1900, Officer Charles Conaway was the first police officer killed by a streetcar. He was saving a female from being hit by the streetcar when he became trapped between two of the trolley cars and was crushed.

He served with the Philadelphia Police Department in Pennsylvania.

Officer Charles Benderoth was the first motorcycle cop to die on duty. He was making a turn and was struck by a passing car. The accident occurred on April 20, 1914. During his recovery he contracted meningitis and died on May 2, 1914. Officer Benderoth served with the St. Louis Police Department in Missouri.

Regardless of the safety precautions and lessons that the police are taught; accidents are bound to happen, typically when responding to calls. On October 7, 2005, Deputy Shadron (Shad) Bassett was responding to a call to save someone who wanted to commit suicide; trying against all odds to reach the intended victim; he became a victim himself. His squad car spun out of control for an unknown reason. It went into a drainage ditch before it struck a tree on the driver's side of the car. The car then took out a huge section of the woods. He was wearing a seatbelt at the time, but he still suffered massive head injuries from the impact and died at the scene. Though he was traveling at speeds of 117 mph; Deputy Bassett was an experienced race car driver so traveling at such a high speed was not uncommon for him. Deputy Shadron Bassett was 34 years old at the time of his death. He served with the Pulaski County Sheriff's Office in Indiana.

On July 24, 1916, Police Matron Anna Hart became the first female correction officer to be killed in the line of duty. She was working as a correction officer and while walking through a section that she deemed secure; she was ambushed by an inmate who was attempting to steal her keys and escape. The prisoner struck Matron Hart with an iron bed post. Matron Hart served with the Hamilton County Sheriff's Department in Ohio.

On December 12, 1971, Police Matron Marta Shanaman, became the first female police officer to be shot and killed in the line of duty. She was shot while preventing a prisoner from breaking out of a correction center. Matron Shanaman served with the Detroit Police Department in Michigan.

On September 20, 1974, Officer Gail Cobb became the first African-American woman to be shot and killed in the line of duty. She was working foot patrol and received a tip that a suspected bank robber was in a nearby garage. Officer Cobb located the suspect and ordered him to place his hands on the wall. While she radioed for back-up he spun back around and shot her. The bullet went through her wrist and her police radio before penetrating in her heart. Officer Cobb served with the Metropolitan Police Department in the District of Columbia.

I wish I could pay homage to each and every law enforcement worker killed in the line of duty because they are all heroes. The following men and women further represent the dangers of their work; the risks they take every day and the sacrifice they made in the end. The sacrifice to keep all of us safe!

Officer Daniel "Danny" Martinez

Arkansas Officer, Daniel Martinez, of the Fort Smith Police Department was shot in the head on the afternoon of March 23, 2007, attempting to assist a mother and child. Earlier that day, the mother had a run-in with an ex-boyfriend, Bobby Englebright, which caused Englebright to be arrested and charged with aggravated assault, battery and false imprisonment. She was returning to the home to retrieve her child and called for the police to accompany her.

She met Officer Martinez in a parking lot. When the two of them knocked on the door, Richard Englebright, brother of the man arrested earlier, answered. He told them to wait a minute, then shut the door. He returned with a 9 mm handgun and shot Officer Martinez in the head. As the mother fled from the scene, he shot her in the back, shoulder and elbow.

Officer Martinez was taken to Sparks Regional Medical Center, where he was pronounced dead. The shooter fled from the home. Oklahoma Highway Patrol officers found him near Spiro, Oklahoma. He committed suicide before officers arrived.

Officer Martinez was a graduate from Poteau High School in Oklahoma. He served with Oklahoma's Poteau Police Department, Panama Police, Shady Point Police and Wister Police Department. He joined the Arkansas Fort Smith Police Department on July 3, 2006.

In Wister, Oklahoma, the section of Highway 270 that runs between Leflore County and Latimer County was named, "The Officer Danny Martinez Memorial Highway." It can usually take up to five years to dedicate a highway but in Officer Martinez situation it only took a matter of weeks. Oklahoma Senator Kenneth Corn explained the reason being "this law enforcement officer gave his life on behalf of the people of our state and, in this case, the state of Arkansas."

Officer Martinez has been forever memorialized by Mike Pratt's memorial "embracelets" at Tatebands.org.

Captain Ike Steele

Sergeant John Dennard

Correction Officer Richard Burke

Correction Officer Donna Fitzgerald

Correction Officer Donna Fitzgerald was stabbed 25 times while on duty at the Tomoka Correctional Institution on June 25, 2008. Her attacker, Enoch Hall, was hiding behind a shed and pounced on Officer Fitzgerald when she approached. The officer was unarmed and was searching for the inmate at the time. He stabbed her with a shank made from a piece of sheet metal.

Officer Fitzgerald was a single mother and was working overtime the night of the savage attack. She served with the Florida Department of Corrections for 13 years.

This was not the first stabbing that the Florida Correctional Institute endured. On October 12, 1980, Correction Officer, Richard Burke, was stabbed while escorting death row inmates from their cells to the shower.

On May 5, 1983, Sergeant John Dennard was viciously attacked and stabbed by two inmates, on the floor of the main housing unit at the Union Correctional Facility. The prisoners were armed with a shank they built. Sergeant Dennard was flown to a local hospital where he died from his injuries. A monument has since been erected in his honor by the Union Correctional Facility.

Detective Dennis Stepnowski

Detective Dennis Carmen Stepnowski was shot in the neck on June 29, 2006 at the Mountain Crest Apartments in Stone Mountain Georgia. Detective Stepnowski and his partner were investigating a burglary in the complex and confronted Lucas Palmer to question him.

Palmer was an evacuee from Hurricane Katrina and wanted on murder charges. When the officers confronted Palmer, he assumed they were there to arrest him for that reason. This caused him to panic and run with the officers fast in pursuit. During the foot chase Palmer opened fire; shooting Detective Stepnowski in the neck with a machine gun type firearm. Though he was fatally wounded, Detective Stepnowski returned fire and killed the suspect. During the shoot-out Palmer was shouting that he wasn't going back to jail. Detective Stepnowski was taken to DeKalb Medical Center in Decatur where he died from his wounds.

Dennis "Step" Stepnowski was a graduate of Lithonia High School in Georgia. After graduating from the police academy, he went on to serve the SWAT team for the Dekalb County, Georgia Police Department. He served as a police officer for 12 years.

He is survived by his wife, Kellie, his parents and his sister, Brandy.

On November 18, 2006 a group of motorcycle enthusiasts hosted the True American Hero Benefit Motorcycle Ride in honor of Detective Stepnowski. John Walsh, of America's Most Wanted, served as Grand Marshal. All proceeds from the ride were donated to the True American Hero Fund in memory of Detective Stepnowski.

Sergeant Mark Renninger

Police Officer Tina Griswold

Police Officer Greg Richards

Police Officer Ronald Owens

Police Officer Tina Griswold, Sergeant Mark Renninger, Officer Greg Richards and Officer Ronald Owens were killed in an ambush style shooting the morning of November 29, 2009 in Lakewood Washington. The officers were sitting inside the coffee shop, Forza Coffee Company, catching up on their paperwork on their laptops before their shifts started. That was when Maurice Clemmons walked in and stood in line to buy coffee. When he reached the counter; without any warning, he pulled out a gun, turned around and began shooting the officers. Two of the officers did not have a chance to respond. As one of the officer's stood up and reached for his weapon he too was shot and killed. The fourth officer struggled with Clemmons all the way to the door before Clemmons shot and killed him. However, that officer was able to fire a few shots at the killer before he fled from the scene. One bullet struck Clemmons in the stomach.

Clemmons only motive that day was that he simply wanted to kill police. The officers were in uniforms at the time that they were murdered. Their marked cars were outside the coffee shop.

Clemmons eluded the police for three days. On December 2nd during the middle of the night, a Seattle officer on patrol spotted a stolen car with the hood up and engine running. He pulled to the side of the road to see what was going on and he was approached by Clemmons. The officer immediately recognized Clemmons and ordered him to stop. Clemmons ignored his order and attempted to pull out a handgun; that he stole from one of the slain officers. The officer shot the suspect and he died at the scene. It was later learned that he would have died soon from the bullet wound he received in the stomach because it was not properly treated.

Officer Tina Griswold, Sergeant Mark Renninger, Officer Greg Richards, and Officer Ronald Owens all served with the Lakewood Police Department in Washington.

Police Officer Michael Crawshaw

Officer Michael Crawshaw, of Penn Hills, Pennsylvania, was shot and killed on December 6, 2009, while answering a domestic call. He was responding to a disturbance call and was parked several doors down from the home, waiting for backup to arrive. When he heard shots fired from inside the home, he unholstered his service weapon and proceeded to exit the vehicle. The assailant emerged from the home, armed with an assault weapon, and shot Officer Crawshaw once in the head and several times in the arm. Officer Crawshaw never had a chance to defend himself. He was not even out of the vehicle yet. It was later learned that the dispute was over a $500 drug debt!

Officer Crawshaw served previously with the University of Pittsburgh's Campus Police but he had a desire to do more for his community, so he left the college and joined the Penn Hills Police Department. His brother, Matthew, serves with the Northern Regional Police Department.

The Pittsburgh Steelers and their fans paid homage to Officer Crawshaw before a game against the Baltimore Ravens on December 27th. The Crawshaw family were in attendance and deeply moved by their tribute.

This was not the first time that Penn Hills Police Department mourned the death of their own. On March 25, 1972, Sergeant Bartley Connolly and Sergeant William Schrott were shot while attempting to stop an armed robbery at a local mall. The officers thought the suspect was a child because the female had a small frame and because of that, their initial reaction was to talk her into disarming her weapon. She shot and killed the officers in cold blood! Sergeant Connolly and Sergeant Schrott will never be forgotten for their compassionate and heroic acts that afternoon.

Police Officer Julius Moore

Officer Julius Moore of the St. Louis Police Department in Missouri, was in a car accident on October 6, 2009 and died from his injuries on October 15th. He was responding to a call to backup up fellow officers who were in pursuit of a burglary suspect. Officer Moore was driving at a high speed; with lights and sirens blaring. There was a tractor trailer traveling in the same direction as Officer Moore. The truck driver decided to make a right turn and when he did this, he crashed into Officer Moore's squad car and pushed it into a brick wall. It is unknown why the driver ignored the officer's lights and sirens.

Officer Moore was 23 years old when he was killed in the accident. He left behind a wife and three young children. Unfortunately, the United States government only goes so far to help families like Officer Moore. Social Security offers survivor benefits to help families but only if they die at a specific age. It doesn't matter that people like Officer Moore didn't have a choice of when he passed on; the government simply sees them as "dying too young." This makes families, like Officer Moore, ineligible for survivor benefits.

Backstoppers, a non-profit group, that helps families of fallen police officers and firefighters, presented a $5,000 check to Officer Moore's wife. Ron Battelle, executive director of Backstoppers, met with the young mother again to review all of her bills. They want to pay off all of her debts. "Our goal is to make them debt-free," Battelle said. "We'll pay off their house, all their other bills, credit card bills, automobile payments. Obviously, she's going to have enough on her mind with three small children. We want her not to have to worry about financial obligations. It takes one little aspect of stress out of her life and allows her to concentrate on raising her children." Backstoppers is now in their 50th year and is funded through donations.

The Third District Business Police Partnership of St Louis Missouri holds an Annual Flag Football Game at their neighborhood Cherokee Park to show support for a variety of organizations in the Third District. The games are played in October by current and former St Louis police officers that have patrolled the 3rd district. They compete against local business owners in the game. Timmy Miller, business owner and board member of the Partnership Program explains that some of the officers have moved on to other departments but return to play homage to the community that gave them their start. The 3rd district is a "very depressed community with high crime and high poverty." The money raised at the football game is donated to groups in the area. The group has helped families with diabetes, they have given money to the boys and girls club and sponsored youth basketball programs. They have also used funds to pass out drug brochures to educate the public. They have plans to build a stone path into the park with a large memorial stone at the head of the path dedicated to Officer Moore.

During past games Officer Julius Moore patrolled the area; keeping everyone safe. In 2009 he was scheduled to play in the game. It was his first year assisting the Partnership program and playing in their flag football game and he was looking forward to it. He was killed less than two weeks prior to the game. The proceeds from their 2009 game were donated to Officer Moore's family. The event featured a military fly-over, fireworks and a performance from the Honor Guards and the Normandy High School band, from where Officer Moore graduated in 2004.

Deputy Sheriff Derek Paul Ward

On July 2, 2004, Deputy Derek Ward, of New York's Allegany County Sheriff's Office, responded to a call in the town of Rushford to assist in a "search and rescue." His police cruiser was struck by a car coming from the opposite direction. The driver not only refused to yield for the officer, but he went through a stop sign before he struck the deputy. Deputy Ward died from his injuries the following day.

Deputy Ward, a 1994 graduate of New York's, Angelica High School, earned two degrees in Criminal Justice, one from Genesse Community College; the other from Brockport State University of New York. He earned his police certification in 1997 at the Rural Police Training Institute. He was proud that his dad was a New York Police Officer and wanted to follow in his footsteps.

His career began as a Patrol Officer with New York's, Angelica Police Department and the Friendship Police Department. He also worked part time as a Correction's Officer with the Allegany County Sheriff' Office. During the last three years of his career he served as a Deputy Sheriff.

He had a fondness for teaching safety and held several positions as an Instructor. As a Multi-Agency Emergency Response Team Firearms Instructor, he taught classes at several gun ranges for most of Allegany County's local police departments. He taught defensive tactics at the Basic Corrections Academy in Allegany County, as well as, Chautauqua and Cattaraugus County. He also served as an instructor for New York Safe Boating.

Following the Attack at the World Trade Center on September 11th, Derek was among a group of officers from the Allegany County PD to assist in the search and rescue of victims.

A hero in life, as well as, death; Deputy Ward's final contribution to society was being an organ donor. His heart was transplanted to a 38-year-old man from New York who had been on the transplant list for three years. His liver was given to a 58-year-old female. One kidney went to a 69-year-old male in Illinois; the other kidney and pancreas went to a 56-year-old male in western New York. Both lungs were given to a 63-year-old male in South Carolina. A 40-year-old male from Buffalo received one of his cornea's. The other was donated to a New York Eye Bank. Bone material was donated to 40-50 patients.

Police Officer Eric Kelly

Police Officer Stephen Mayhle

Police Officer Paul Sciullo II

Pittsburgh Police Officers Stephen Mayhle, Paul Sciullo II and Eric Kelly were shot and killed in what is now known as the "Pittsburgh Tragedy." On April 4, 2009, Officer Mayhle and Officer Sciullo responded to a domestic dispute between a mother and son. The officers were misinformed and told that there were no weapons involved. As they approached the door they were ambushed. Both officers were shot in the head and died at the scene.

Officer Kelly was off duty but when he heard the call on the radio, he too went to the home to assist. Still in his uniform when he arrived, he saw his fallen brothers in front of the door of the home and rushed to go to their aid. He was shot as he exited his squad car.

Though he was fatally wounded, Officer Kelly was able to radio for back-up and inform officers of their location and what was happening. When back-up officers arrived, they tried to retrieve the fallen officers but in each attempt; the assailant, who was barricaded inside the home, would shoot at them. The subject was heavily armed and firing high powered assault weapons at the officers.

When Officer Timothy McManaway got close to Officer Kelly, the assailant shot Officer McManaway in the hand. Officer Brian Jones jumped a fence in an attempt to retrieve Officer Kelly and broke his leg in the fall. Officers were successful in their attempts to retrieve Officer Kelly from the scene. Officer Kelly died at the hospital from his wounds.

Over 100 police officers and FBI agents swarmed the scene. During the 4-hour standoff, the subject was shot several times in the legs and vest (he was wearing a bullet proof vest). Utility crews cut off the power to the killer's home to assure he was not following media reports.

When the shooter surrendered officers retrieved him from

the home without incident. A reporter asked, "How can you bring him out alive when he just killed three police officers?" To which the officer responded, "That's the difference between him and us."

At a memorial service for the officers, Chief Nate Harper of the Pittsburgh police said, "April 4, 2009, was truly the darkest day in the Pittsburgh Bureau of Police." He presented plaques of remembrance to the families of each officer. Each of the officers served with the Pittsburgh Police Department in Pennsylvania.

Memorial shirts were made to commemorate the sacrifices of Officers Stephen Mayhle, Paul Sciullo II and Eric Kelly. The shirts were designed by Detective Patrick Moffatt and approved by Chief Harper. Proceeds from the sale of the shirts were given to the Pittsburgh Fallen Heroes Fund.

Officer Mary Lynn Beall

On May 15, 2000, Officer Mary Lynn Beall was shot and paralyzed when she responded to a domestic dispute. She was attempting to make a peaceful negotiation with the subject to spare him from being injured. In response, he shot her, execution style. She was among a group of officers who responded to a call of a man shooting at his girlfriend. Officer Beall confronted the subject and tried to talk him into surrendering. She knelt before him and re-holstered her weapon. At that point the subject stuck his gun into her neck and fired.

It was later found that the shooter, Raham Twitty, bought his gun from a gun show, which was an illegal sale because, at the time, Twitty was under indictment.

Officer Beall was left paralyzed from the neck down and underwent more than ten surgeries within two years from the day of the incident. On August 25, 2002, Officer Beall died from complications that stemmed from the shooting.

Officer Beall served with the Dayton Police Department in Ohio for three years. Her husband is with the Dayton Police Department today.

Officer Robert Winget

On April 10, 2007, dispatch received an inaudible message from Officer Winget but were unable to make further contact with him. A search and rescue team gathered to search for him. They found Officer Winget 90 minutes later. He was patrolling in a heavily wooded area near the Stanislaus River when he wrecked his ATV. He passed away several hours later from the injuries he sustained.

Officer Winget was a Marine Corps veteran and fought in the Vietnam War. He served the Los Angeles Police Department for 20 years and the Stanislaus County Sheriff's Office for 14 years. At Stanislaus he worked in patrol, as a bailiff and as a DARE (Drug Awareness Resistance Education) Officer. Senator Dave Cogdill awarded him for his DARE lessons. He was an assemblyman at the time.

FROM FELLOW OFFICER GORDON WEST

It was the first, and hopefully last time, that I had to see a partner on a backboard getting CPR. He was in Vietnam, was a cop for over 35 years. He had been shot at and stabbed, and an ATV killed him! At that time, I was in charge of the Honor Guard. I had to help put together all the arrangements for his service. It has been over a year and a half since the accident, but there isn't a day goes by that I don't think about Bob and how he affected the department. He was a great cop, and he is greatly missed.

STATEMENT FROM ARNOLD SCHWARZENEGGER

Officer Winget put his life on the line to protect the safety of our citizens. Robert's tremendous bravery and selfless dedication to our communities is an inspiration to all Californians. Maria and I extend our heartfelt sympathies to Robert's family, friends and fellow officers as they mourn this tragic loss.

School Safety Agent Vivian Samuels-Benjamin

On December 16, 2005, School Safety Agent Vivian Samuels-Benjamin suffered a fatal heart attack when a rowdy student assaulted her. Agent Samuels was serving with the New York City Police Department's Division of School Safety and was asked to work at a school dance in Crown Heights, Brooklyn. As students were entering the building, a 12-year-old began to cause a disturbance. Agent Samuels denied the student admission and attempted to escort her from the building. The student then attacked Agent Samuels by kicking her and punching her in the head twice; knocking the agent to the ground. Agent Samuels was able to stand back up but moments later she collapsed. She was taken to Kings County Hospital where she died from a heart attack brought on from the punches.

Agent Samuels was dedicated to protecting the children of New York city schools. She proudly served as a School Safety Agent for the New York City Police Department for 24 years.

Corporal Scott Severns

On April 21, 2006 Corporal Scott Severns was shot and killed during an attempted robbery while he was off duty. He was walking to his car with a friend when a masked gunman ran towards them in a robbery attempt. Corporal Severns stepped in front of his friend and pushed her to the ground. Corporal Severns put his hands in the air; attempting to calm the situation and prevent anyone from getting hurt. A second suspect driving a getaway car emerged on the scene. When one of the suspects pulled out a gun and began firing; the corporal reached for his gun and was able to wound one of the assailants but was shot several times himself. Corporal Severns died two days later from four gunshot wounds he received that day.

Corporal Severns was a decorated police officer. He received the Chief's Award of Valor and was named Officer of the Year in 2004.

Every year in early July, the Blackthorn Golf Course hosts the Annual Scott Severns Memorial Golf Outing. The proceeds from the outing are donated to Indiana's Southlawn Cemetery. They are reconstructing a corner of the cemetery into the "Police and Fallen Heroes" section; in honor of Corporal Scott Severns. Corporal Severns was 36 years old at the time of his death. He served with the South Bend Police Department in Indiana.

Deputy Vernon Matthew Williams

On September 28, 2006, Deputy Vernon Matthew Williams (affectionately known as "Matt") and his K9 partner DiOGi (pronounced dee-oh-gee) were both shot and killed while searching for a suspect that ran during a traffic stop.

Deputy Speirs initially stopped the vehicle for a traffic violation and the suspect then fled on foot to nearby woods. Deputy Williams then arrived with his K9 to assist Deputy Speirs in searching for the suspect. As DiOGi zeroed in on the suspect he opened fire killing the K9 instantly. He then shot Deputy Williams eight times. Speirs, who was searching in another area of the woods, was also shot in the leg during the search.

When Deputy Williams failed to respond to officers calls on the radio; the Polk County K9 Teams were brought in to search for him. They were aware of the armed suspect shooting at officers but also knew they had to face those dangers to find Deputy Williams. They located their fallen brother who was deceased by then and brought him out of the woods.

Several hours later the shooter emerged from the woods and fired at a Lakewood police officer who was warning residents to stay clear of the area and why. He missed the officer and went back into the woods.

The next morning the shooter was still hiding in the woods and there were nearly 500 officers and K9 Teams scouring the area looking for the suspect. Shortly before 10:00 AM, SWAT moved in a line formation through the wooded area and located the assailant hiding under a tree that was knocked over in a previous storm. When he refused to surrender and pulled Deputy Williams' handgun out on the SWAT team he was shot and killed him.

Deputy Williams was a K9 handler for 8 years. He was 39 years old at the time of his death. He served with the Polk County Sheriff's Office in Florida. Shortly before his death he started his own dog obedience and training business.

Officer Eric Zapata

Deputy Sheriff Sherri Jones

On April 18, 2011, the law enforcement community would suffer the loss of two officers on opposite directions of the country. Deputy Sheriff Sherri Jones was shot and killed, in the basement of the Bowie County Courthouse in Texas while moving a prisoner from the courtroom to a transport van. During the scuffle, the prisoner overpowered Deputy Jones and gained control of her gun. He shot Deputy Jones in the head and stole the transport van. He escaped to Arkansas where he was captured at a convenience store.

Nine hours later in Kalamazoo, Michigan, Officer Eric Zapata, was shot and killed when answering to a call for "shots fired" in a residential neighborhood. When the officers arrived at the scene, Zapata's partner saw Leonard Statler and simply asked him if he heard any gun shots. Statler pulled a gun and fired at the officer. Statler then fled on foot, running down the alley, in the direction of Officer Zapata. He shot Officer Zapata in the chest with a high powered rife.

Officer Zapata was a member of the Lightning Kicks Martial Arts, a martial arts training center, where he volunteered as a mentor for the youth. His passion was playing golf and his final Facebook post said, "Life is a game, but golf is serious."

Deputy Sheriff Ethan Collins

On January 4, 2006, Deputy Ethan Collins of the Fairfield County Sheriff's Office was killed in an automobile accident when he responded to assist a fellow officer, who was engaged in a fight with a juvenile. The teen was in possession of a razor and was threatening suicide. While en route, Deputy Collins lost control of his cruiser on State Route 188 and died on the scene.

Several honors have been made in tribute to Deputy Collins, the first being a scholarship in his name; that was started by his family. The scholarship is available to those in Fairfield County, Ohio who are interested in becoming a police officer. The money can also be used by current law enforcement workers who wish to further their education.

The portion of State Route 188 that extends through Fairfield County was renamed "The Deputy Ethan Collins Memorial Highway."

Officer Terry Gatewood served alongside Deputy Collins and knew the officer well. Gatewood was also a Boy Scout leader for Pack 227. The children in his scout troop were saddened over the officer's death and stressed a desire to want to do something in honor of Deputy Collins. They just weren't sure the best way to do this. They had a group discussion and tossed around ideas, including raising money for Deputy Collins family. Gatewood suggested they focus more on an activity that would honor his memory.

The troop soon learned that Deputy Collins was being honored at the Fallen Officers Memorial Ceremony in Washington, DC. They knew immediately they wanted to be there! The next step was to raise money for the trip. A little determination goes a long way for a boy scout troop with a goal!

In the year that followed, Pack 227 set out on a series of a fundraising projects that included car washes, donut sales, rock-a-thons and pancake breakfasts. Gatewood jokes that they "probably invented a few fund raisers along the way." The fundraisers combined weren't enough to raise the money for the trip. It was donations from the community that made up the difference. The troop had enough money for a hotel stay, transportation costs and even a few site seeing tours.

Officer Terry Gatewood: One of my favorite memories was when we went to the candlelight vigil the night before the ceremony and there were so many officers, family and citizens there that the scouts couldn't see what was happening. Then a Lieutenant from the Seattle Police Department saw one of the scouts and picked him up and put him up high, so he could see. Then other officers saw that and before you knew it the scouts were being hoisted up, high in the air.

Because of their actions in 2006 and 2007, the Scouts of Pack 227 were allowed to do something that, to my knowledge, has not been allowed in scouting before: they were allowed by the National Council of the Boy Scouts of America to affix an "End of Watch" pin for Deputy Ethan Collins to their uniforms permanently – a pin unique to Pack 227, a pin that no other pack or troop wears.

FROM FELLOW OFFICER TERRY GATEWOOD

Ethan had a great sense of humor and sense of duty and made the ultimate sacrifice doing the job he loved. He was a great husband, father and friend and his passing leaves a tremendous void in the law enforcement family. Rest in peace my brother, we've got it from here...

Officer Michael Edward Deno

Officer Mike Deno was shot and killed on February 29, 2000 when he pulled Richard Branum over for driving with a suspended license. During the traffic stop, Branum, pulled out a .25 caliber handgun from his rear pocket and shot Officer Deno in the head.

Branum fled the scene but was arrested an hour later by Gibson County Sheriff's Deputies without incident. During his arrest, they found that Branum had drugs taped under his clothing.

Officer Deno was transported to Saint Mary's Medical Center in Evansville, Indiana, where he died the next morning from his injuries. Officers from across the country, as well as, Canada's Royal Mounted Police attended Officer Deno's funeral services. During the hours of Officer Deno's funeral the town completely shut down out of respect to their fallen officer.

It was when Mike Deno was nineteen years old that he decided to pursue a career in public services. He was a 1994 graduate of Indiana's, Waldo J Wood Memorial High School. When he was traveling to Kentucky with his father to visit his brother (who was in the military) they came across a terrible car accident. They jumped from their car to assist in the rescue and Mike was credited with saving the driver's life. From then on, he knew that he wanted to serve his community and do everything possible to protect others in danger. Later that year, his step father, Tom Bonilla, encouraged him to join the Oakland City Fire Department, where Bonilla was also a member.

Officer Deno came from a close-nit family and enjoyed working on cars with his father, Melvin, and brother, Matt. He even spent time with his mother, dusting the house while the two listened to John Denver music.

His first job in law enforcement was with the Oakland City Police Department in 1998. He first served as a Reserve Officer and later as a part time Patrol Officer. On August 20, 1999, he graduated from the Indiana Law Enforcement

Academy and was sworn in as a full-time officer. That year, he went on to Oakland City University where he was continuing his education in Criminal Justice.

Since his death Officer Deno's wife, Cindy, established the Michael Edward Deno Memorial Fund. A scholarship for seniors graduating from Oakland City University in the Criminal Justice Field.

Officer Deno's badge number (#25-5) was retired from his department to honor the fallen officer.

His name was added to the Gibson County Fallen Heroes Monument, as well as the Wall of Remembrance in Washington, D.C and the Indiana Law Enforcement and Firefighters Memorial. In May 2003, The Oakland City Fallen Heroes Monument was erected on the front lawn of the Oakland City Fire Department, with Officer Mike Deno's name included.

Officer Derek Kotecki

On October 12, 2011, Officer Derek Kotecki, was shot and killed trying to catch a fugitive, wanted on drug-related charges. The harrowing incident took place outside of a Dairy Queen in New Kensington, Pennsylvania. Once again showing the public that the men in blue; truly do put their lives between the public and the criminals who want to do them harm.

Officer Kotecki was a K9 officer who was one week shy of his18th year in law enforcement. He worked with the DARE Program and influenced a number of children in the Lower Burrell area. He was a friend to everyone who met him, a hero to the community, particularly the children, and he even tried to aid the people he arrested.

Kelly Kotecki-Stephenson: If there was a person on drugs and Derek arrested that person, he'd talk some sense into that person, like it was his friend he was talking to.

The community paid their respect to the fallen officer by tying ribbons along Leechurg Road and businesses posted signs showing messages of sorrow and condolence to the Kotecki family. The Lower Burrell Volunteer Fire Company #1 and the Saddle Up Band held a fundraiser for the Kotecki family and raised $7,500.

Lower Burrell Patrolman Tom Babinsack: Remember, it is not how he died that made him a hero. It was how he lived.

A website has also been created in honor of the officer: OfficerKotecki.com

Officer Timothy Brenton

Officer Timothy Brenton was shot and killed on October 31, 2009, while sitting in his patrol car. He was the passenger in his squad car and was working with a trainee. They were discussing a traffic stop that they just completed; when the assailant pulled alongside their car and opened fire. There was no reason for this; he simply shot and killed Officer Brenton in a cowardly ambush!

Officer Brenton died at the scene and the trainee was grazed in the back when she ducked from the spray of bullets. She was able to jump from her car and return fire. She was also able to radio for back-up.

It was during Officer Brenton's memorial service that officers received a tip on the location of the shooter. While they were attempting to arrest him; he pulled a gun out on those officers as well.

Officer Timothy Brenton served with the Seattle Police Department in Washington. It has been said that Officer Brenton wanted to be a police officer since he was a child playing "cops and robbers." His father and uncle are retired Seattle police officers. He is remembered for his dedication as well as his great sense of humor during tense situations.

A former partner of his recalled one of those situations. They had pulled over a stolen SUV and found that the driver was a nervous juvenile. As they were talking to him, Officer Brenton reached inside the vehicle and held up a handgun. He then said, "Uh oh, what's this?" The nervous teen started freaking out. Officer Brenton responded with "Oh wait, this one's mine" and put it back in his holster.

Mayor Greg Nickels: Officer Brenton is a homegrown hero. He didn't set out to be a hero.

Governor Chris Gregoire: On behalf of all the people of the state of Washington, I thank Officer Brenton and his family and his fellow officers. We will cherish his memory always. As Officer Brenton demonstrated, putting on the uniform is an act of courage every day, every time. His death was tragic. It was unjust. But we will not allow the unthinkable circumstances of his death to overshadow his life of service. His service was noble, it was selfless. It was for the cause of justice. He encouraged the absolute best in all those who wear the uniform and assumed the risk for all of us.

Judgment Day for a Police Officer

The policeman stood and faced his God; which must always come to pass. He hoped his shoes were shining; just as brightly as his brass.

"Step forward now, Policeman; How shall I deal with you? Have you always turned the other cheek? To my Church have you been true?"

The policeman squared his shoulders and said; "No, Lord I guess I ain't, because those of us who carry badges; can't always be a Saint."

I've had to work most Sundays and at times my work was rough, and sometimes I've been violent; because the streets are awfully tough.

But I never took a penny; that wasn't mine to keep. I worked a lot of overtime; when the bills just got too steep.

And I never passed a cry for help; though at times I shook with fear. And sometimes, God forgive me; I've wept unmanly tears.

I know I don't deserve a place; among the people here. They never wanted me around; except to calm their fear. If you've a place for me here, Lord; It needn't be so grand. I never expected or had too much but if you don't, I'll understand."

There was silence all around the Throne; where the Saints had often trod. As the policeman waited quietly, for the judgment of his God.

"Step forward now, policeman, you've borne your burdens well. Come walk a beat on Heaven's streets; you've done your time in Hell."

As you close this chapter.... these officers now becoming a name on a page to you, remember, whether their death was in 1983 or last month, they are never forgotten by those who love them. Their memories and faces are emblazoned on the hearts of family, friends and a community who miss them just as much today as the day they heard the words...End of Watch.

Section III

A Blue Tribute

There are over 50,000 assaults against law enforcement every year. California has had more "line of duty deaths" than any other state. Vermont has had the fewest. The deadliest day in Law Enforcement was September 11, 2001 when 72 officers were killed. The toxic fumes in the air led to the death of many more law enforcement workers in the years that followed.

The National Law Enforcement Memorial

In 1962, President John Kennedy declared May 15 to be National Peace Officers Memorial Day and the week in which it falls will be National Police Week.

The National Law Enforcement Memorial was presented to the public on October 15, 1991. President George W. Bush made that day National Law Enforcement Memorial Dedication Day. A wreath laying ceremony is held every year in dedication of the fallen officers.

On January 3, 1791 Constable Darius Quimby, of the Albany County Constable's Office, in New York, was shot and killed while attempting to arrest a man on a trespass warrant. The subject who killed Quimby was found guilty of the murder and hanged on August 26, 1791. Constable Quimby is the first law enforcement worker in the United States to be killed in the line of duty. His name has not yet been added to the Memorial Wall.

On May 17, 1792 Deputy Sheriff Isaac Smith, of the Westchester County Sheriff's Department in New York, was the first police officer killed in the line of duty. He was responding to a disturbance call at "The Hunt's Inn." John Ryer was unruly and argued with other customers and the tavern's owner asked for the deputy's help in removing him from the premises. In doing so, the officer was shot the officer to death by Ryer. Deputy Smith was a veteran of the Revolutionary War. On May 14, 2000, his name was added to the National Law Enforcement Memorial.

On July 24, 1916, Ohio Prison Matron, Anna Hart, of the Hamilton County Sheriff's Office became the first female to die in the line of duty. She was beaten to death by a prisoner during an escape attempt. He was armed with an iron bed post.

The American Police Hall of Fame and Museum

The American Police Hall of Fame and Museum was first established in North Port, Florida in 1960. In 1988 it was relocated to Miami and its final move was to Titusville in 2003. The Hall of Fame was added to the museum in 1998. They receive annual nominations to the Hall of Fame through citizens, police departments and the advisory board members.

The museum, which is 50,000 square feet, consists of over 11,000 artifacts is an educational timeline on the history of law enforcement. One section of the museum consists of automobiles used in law enforcement and in the movies; including a car from "Bladerunner." There is a section dedicated to law enforcement in the wild west. The museum is so chalk full of displays and activities that guests are guaranteed a fun-pack-filled day when they visit. They can take helicopter rides, sit in an electric chair, watch a canine display, operate a drunk driving simulator, observe an authentic crime lab and assist in the crime solving. There is also a gun range that is open to the pubic 6 days a week.

There is a marble wall displayed with the names of American police officers who have fallen. Each year the museum hosts "Police Memorial Week" and the names of fallen officers from the previous year are added to the wall.

Located inside the museum are the offices of the National Association of Chiefs of Police and the American Federation of Police and Concerned Citizens. These offices assist the needs of police departments throughout the country. They have helped smaller departments with the costs of K9 dogs by donating grants of up to $5,000 to help cover the expenses of a K9 police dog. K9s are extremely beneficial to police departments, in which they assist in drug seizures, arrests and missing people searches. Many of the departments receiving the grants are working with their first K9 or they are smaller departments adding on to their police force. Police departments across the country are welcome to apply. No one has been turned down so far.

PDPOF scholarships, of up to $500 a year for 4 years are offered to rehabilitate police officers injured on duty. It can be used to further their education or pay medical costs. They also established the PDPOF Gift Program. They send Birthday and Christmas gifts to the officer and his family to show them that their sacrifice to the community of law enforcement will never be forgotten.

When a police officer falls in the line of duty they step up and do all they can to assist the officer's family. They see to it that the family receives a "Line of Duty Death Package" within 48 hours of the officer's death. The package includes a $1,000 check to assist in any needed immediate expenses, as well as, literature that describes each of their programs. There is the "Family Survivor Scholarship Program" that offers $1,000 a year for 4 years to the children of police officers who are killed in the line of duty.

There is the "Family Survivor Gift Program" that sends birthday and Christmas presents, as well as, gifts on Father's/Mother's Day. There are "Summer Camp Scholarships" for children who wish to attend summer camp. They are awarded $200 each.

They also send a Posthumous Medal of Honor, certificate, Memorial Flag and letter to the department of the fallen officer. "Flowers of Remembrance" are sent to the officer's department in the first two years that follow their death.

Police Unity Tour

The Police Unity Tour was established to raise money for The National Law Enforcement Officers Memorial (NLEOM). A group of cyclists ride from Florham Park in New Jersey to the National Law Enforcement Officers Memorial in Washington DC. The Police Unity Tour was the idea of Officer Patrick Montuore in an attempt to raise awareness of the sacrifices of police officers. The first ride was in 1997 and 18 police officers participated. They now have over 1,000 participants. In 2005 they pledged 5 million dollars of support to the National Law Enforcement Museum. Law enforcement from across the country now participate in the Police Unity Tour. The group's motto is "We ride for those who died."

Move Over America

MOVE OVER AMERICA, is the movement sweeping across the country to gain recognition for the "Move Over" Law. It requires drivers to "move over" when they see a police car along the side of the road performing a traffic stop. It used to be common courtesy that is not the case anymore.

Sergeant Jesse Buttram, of the Lenoir City Police Department in Tennessee, was one of many officers killed by the negligence of drivers refusing to yield for the police. On August 31, 1972 Officer Buttram had just completed a traffic stop when he was struck by another car. The driver of the car that he initially pulled over was a doctor and he tried to save Buttram's life but was unsuccessful. Officer Buttram died that same day of severe head injuries.

Officer Christy Jo Dedman was also killed in the same manner. On July 19, 2004, Dedman was helping a stranded motorist change a flat tire on Interstate 40 in Nashville Tennessee. The lights on her squad car were flashing but this was ignored by the driver of a tractor trailer. He struck the back of her police car; pushing it forward; and causing it to wreck into Dedman and the motorist. At the time of impact, they were both standing in front of the driver's side of the squad car, near a retaining wall. The truck driver was driving at a high speed and in a reckless manner. The driver of the truck had a history of driving reckless. He was only made to serve 9 months in jail. Within two weeks of his release he was arrested again for reckless driving. Officer Dedman served with the Metro Nashville Police Department in Nashville Tennessee.

On November 24, 2006, Senior Trooper Robert Hill, of the Virginia State Police, was killed while conducting a traffic stop. While he was speaking to the driver of the vehicle another car drifted from the travel lane and wrecked into the officer killing him instantly. On June 17, 2008, in honor of Trooper Hill, a bridge in Southampton Virginia was renamed the Senior Trooper Robert A. Hill Bridge.

Since 1791, there have been 776 police officers killed in this manner. The campaign for "Move Over America" started on July 2, 2007, when the Keene Police Officer's Association in New Hampshire joined forces with the National Safety Commission to pass the law nationwide. According to the National Law Enforcement Officers Memorial, since 1997, there have been more than 150 law enforcement officers killed after being struck by vehicles along America's highways, which is the largest spike in these types of deaths in our country's history.

The eight remaining states who have yet to pass the "Move Over" law are: Nebraska, Hawaii, Maryland, Washington DC, New Jersey, Connecticut, Rhode Island and Massachusetts.

Heroes on Patrol

A Rolling Memorial and Tribute

Phil Talpers

The "Rolling Memorial" is a 2001 Ford Crown Victoria with less than 10,000 miles on it. The car has a unique custom hand air brushed paint job, with the front and sides bearing a beautiful American Flag, a large Eagle in the center of the hood, surrounded by 4 ghosted eagles, and stars. In 72 of those stars are the names of the fallen officers from 9/11. In the eye of the eagle is the reflection of the Statue of Liberty who watches over these fallen heroes and those who continue to serve and protect. Moving down the side of the car is an amazing red section of the flag, with tremendous detail of shadows. On the trunk is a beautiful rendition of the New York skyline and a tribute to the World Trade Towers.

The vision dream of this car has been to tribute the fallen multi agency Law Enforcement agents who lost their lives in the World Trade Towers on 9/11/01 trying to unselfishly save others, send a crystal clear thank you to the law enforcement officers that continue to serve, protect and keep us safe, and who have an otherwise thankless job. The Rolling Memorial show the utmost respect for them, and helps share the grief with the survivors of these and other fallen officers. Not enough is done for the Police and we have decided to carry on the mission that began in a small Louisiana town by a former Auxiliary Law Enforcement Officer. He had the original dream, and unfortunately could not properly fund this vision and that is how I got involved.

Our Heroes on Patrol 9/11 commemorative car played an integral role in National Police Week 2004 in Washington DC and we are deeply honored to have been able to share this moving event with the Officers from all over the world who attended and thank all of the thousands of officers, family members and others who took the time to share the experience with us. Watch for my Rolling Memorial in Washington DC for the upcoming National Police Week 2005

Since Police Week 2004 we have had the honor and privilege to take part in many other events. We played a role in Rolling Thunder with the Combat Veterans Motorcycle club giving escort to the pentagon, attended many local regional DARE Events, multiple law enforcement agency events, Police car club meets, and we cannot ever forget the official 911 Ride to New York City where the car made its first official entry into New York and ground zero. Talk about amazing, emotional and fulfilling.

We had a few thousand motorcycles behind us from DC to New York and about 400 Police Bikes from all over the country and of course who could forget the Ontario Provincial Police, leading us in to the WTC area. While in New York we took the car to NYPD HQ and Port Authority Police to share the car with some of the officers who have friends and loved ones being remembered in the stars on the car. While in New York, Port Authority Police took us on a tour of the warehouse where items pulled from the WTC site were housed and until you walk next to the beams or see the burned up Fire Engines, and see the sadness in the faces of the officers telling you of their personal stories and losses it really brings the whole experience to a peak. Our hearts go out to these officers and survivors. This is why we carry this car onward, we will never forget....

Christmas Patrol
Sergeant Don Burns

Christmas Patrol was written by Sergeant Don Burns of the Norfolk Virginia Police Department. He was inspired to write the poem on a Christmas morning that he *was not* scheduled to work. His wife pointed out that in the 16 years they had been married, this was only the third time that he had Christmas Day off. The poem recognizes the sacrifices of law officers and their families.

Christmas Patrol

The town's all aglow with tinsel and light,
A blanket of snow makes even dismal look bright.
While working a wreck, the injured low moan,
I can't help my thoughts from drifting to home.
The kids were excited, when I left them last night,
Each opened one present, their faces all bright.
Tucked them in bed, a big hug for me,
Assembled two bikes, put them under the tree.
Two hours of sleep, a kiss for the wife,
I slipped out the door, this Christmas Eve night.
The medics arrive, strobes flashing with light,
As it turns the next corner, coming into my sight.
Snap back to the present, can't let myself pout,
These people are injured, we must get them out.
As the patients are loaded, I let myself drift,
Totaling up, my own Christmas list.
Two family disputes, a drunk at a bar,
Two missing kids, now this wrecked car.
Call out a wrecker, complete the report,
Fill out my notes, preparing for court.
A trip to the hospital, blood tests are drawn,
Drunk driving's a crime, even this morn.
Quick stop at the station, no time to talk shop,
Santa comes for Christmas, but daddy's still a cop.

Peace of Mind Bracelets

"Peace of Mind" bracelets are designed to honor fallen police officers and fire fighters. The bracelets were the idea off Shannon Schoon. On January 10, 2005, tragedy struck her sister and brother-in-law, Heather and Matt Thomas. Matt's sister, Molly Thomas Bowden was shot and killed during a traffic stop. During the stop, when Officer Bowden approached the driver of the vehicle, the 23-year-old man, shot her in the shoulder. She retreated to the rear of the vehicle for cover. The driver then jumped from the car and shot officer Bowden again in the neck. When she fell to the ground, he shot her two more times in the neck. She died from her injuries a month later on February 10th. Her husband is also a police officer and continues to serve the Columbia Police Department in Ohio; where his wife served for 3 ½ years.

During the month that followed the shooting a charity was started to assist the family with their medical and necessary costs. The bracelet, which Shannon called "Molly's Courage" showcases her badge number and a sterling silver "courage" charm. Shannon initially planned on donating $10 from the sale of each bracelet. When Officer Bowden passed away the money was then used to help start a scholarship for future female police officers.

Shannon: Not long after that bracelet became popular, I started getting requests by other family and friends of fallen officers and service men and women, as well as, other charities such as childhood cancers. All of the charity items on my website began with that first "Molly's Courage" bracelet.

Tye Bands

"Tye Bands" are memorial "embracelets" made to honor police officers, fire fighters and soldiers who have passed away. Tye bands were the creative idea of Mike Pratt Sr. He calls the bands "embracelets" because he feels they are more than jewelry; they are memorials that can be worn all the time. Mike Pratt is the father of slain Officer Jason "Tye" Pratt. On September 11, 2003, Officer Pratt, of the Omaha Nebraska Police Department, was shot and killed in the line of duty. He and several officers were searching for a man who fled on foot from a traffic stop. The suspect peered from the bushes behind Officer Pratt and shot him in the head. He was in a coma for a week and died on September 19th.

Mike Pratt refers to the Tye bands as "the bands that tie them all together." In the beginning he made Tye bands to honor his son's sacrifice. It has since grown into a business that honors fallen officers from around the world, as well as, fallen firefighters and soldiers who were killed at war. Mike Pratt has also started making Tye bands for those who have lossed loved ones and wish to cherish their memory. In his attempts to heal his broken heart from his son's death, he has helped 1,000's more around the world!

Mike Pratt also makes Tye bands for soldiers, firefighters and police officers who are living and serve this country from day-to-day. The men and women on these bands are known as "Standing Heroes."

Mike: God helped me do this, I'm not that sharp to figure this out, I comforted thousands of people...there's something special about seeing the image of the person that you love.

He offers funding to offset the costs for the people who can't afford the Tye Bands. The profits from the bands are donated to a number of organizations and charities each year.

The Perfect Cop

(This was written by a police officer who wanted to give people a taste of what their job entails)

To a Police Chief, the perfect cop is someone who looks sharp, works hard and doesn't expect overtime pay, makes good arrests without offending anyone, writes detailed reports and keeps a neat, readable activity log. He is also always available when extra help is needed, accepts work assignments willingly and comes up with fast, favorable results. In short, a perfect cop is someone who makes the Chief look good.

To a Prosecuting Attorney, a perfect cop is a meticulous investigator who gathers and documents evidence, obtains confessions to all crimes and outlines each case to make the prosecutor's job easy. He doesn't object when a case is plea bargained so the attorneys can go golfing Friday afternoon. He doesn't mind if an offender gets probation or a suspended sentence because it is more convenient to make a deal than go to trial.

To a Defense Attorney, a perfect cop is a bungling idiot who makes mistakes; someone the defense attorney can manipulate and make angry in court, making the attorney look good in front of his client. A perfect cop is someone who will agree to any and all plea bargaining proposed, and whom the defense attorney can call when he needs protection from his own client.

To the City Council, a perfect cop is someone who does his job well without making waves, who is so grateful for a job that he willingly works nights, weekends and holidays. He never asks for more than the city is willing to pay, does an exemplary job without adequate equipment and tools. And he never writes tickets on any council member or their kid.

To the People of the Community, a perfect cop is polite, a friendly person who walks the beat and checks out strange noises and watches for strange people. He teaches kids right from wrong, talks to them about the evils of drug use- but doesn't mention Mom and Dad using alcohol. He will arrest drug dealers but overlooks kids with a "little" pot.

To his Wife, a perfect cop never lets his job effect his emotions. He can spend hours dealing with drunks, domestics, drug users, injured or dead people, and then come home and be a loving, well-adjusted husband and father.

I have been a cop for over 20 years, and have never met a perfect cop. Only a few have even come close, being totally honest and truly caring about people and doing the best job they can. But all the cops I have ever known are human. They love, laugh, cry, hurt, and sometimes die too young. They try to make it to retirement, although many do not. Divorce is common. Some become alcoholics, and some suffer from "police stress", seen in a variety of emotional disorders or heart attacks. Our job is often described as 98% boredom and 2% sheer terror.

Why do we do it? We don't really know. I hope it's because we simply care about right and wrong.

What Cops Know

(And want you to know)

Watch out for the CSI effect. There is no machine that we can drop an eyelash into and come up with the DNA profile, fingerprints, and mug shot of the owner in 2 minutes.

When you see an emergency vehicle behind you with its lights and sirens on: pull to the RIGHT and Stop. We are usually required to pass cars on the left.

Dunkin' Donuts has much better coffee than they do donuts.

When you're driving in the fast lane and you see a cop behind you don't go 5 mph's under the speed limit. We are not impressed by how safe of a driver you can be, we're trying to go help someone or catch that guy in the SUV that just cut you off. Safely move over and let us pass.

If you get a warning instead of a ticket from a cop go buy a lottery ticket, because you've already beaten the odds.

When you see an officer conducting a traffic stop, or with a suspect in handcuffs, it is generally not a good idea to approach the officer and ask for directions. If you do this, don't expect the officer to be nice. You may be told to "get lost."

Yes, if a cop causes a car accident, we usually get a ticket and sometimes we get suspended. When is the last time you got 3 days off, without pay, for rear-ending a guy at Wal-mart?

If you think you can fan all the pot smoke out of the car before we smell it, good luck!

If you are drinking and driving, we know you've had more than two beers. I've never had two beers and driven my car through the front doors of a Toys-R-Us, pissed my pants and passed out with my foot on the gas.

Here's how to get out of a ticket, don't break the law in the first place!

If you drive a piece of junk car; this is why you're getting pulled over. In one week I pulled over 10 cars for minor equipment violations and 8 out of 10 had no vehicle insurance, 7 out of 10 had suspended drivers licenses, 5 out of 10 had warrants, 2 out of 10 had felony warrants, and 1 out of 10 was a known sex offender with his 12 year old niece in the car without her mother's knowledge.

Of the "2 out of 10" that didn't have any other violations, one was given a fix-it-ticket and the other was given a warning and if you are trying to do the math many had multiple violations.

If you've just been pulled over for doing 70 in a 35, do not greet the officer with, "What seems to be the problem, officer?"

We get coffee breaks too, and sometimes we run into stores and do some shopping during them.

When you're the victim of a burglary take the time, you spend waiting for the officer to find the model numbers and the serial numbers of the stuff that was taken.

Yes, some cops are just jerks but take heart in the fact that other cops don't like them either.

If it is nighttime and you're driving a vehicle with tinted windows and I pull you over, it's not because of your skin color. I can't tell if the vehicle even has a driver until the windows are rolled down.

Cops make mistakes and sometimes they are big mistakes.

Some cops are bad and sometimes they're really bad, though most are heroic. Keep in mind, every time you hear on the news about people running away from a crazed gunman, someone's son or daughter in a blue uniform is running TOWARD that crazed gunman.

Yes, it's true, cops usually don't give other cops speeding tickets. Think of it as an employee discount, perk or benefit and unless you're a habitual speeder all you ever get is a fine anyway.

If your local police agency has a helicopter everyone knows it's loud and annoying, but did you know it can cover the same area as 15-20 patrol officers and safely chase criminals that are driving 90 MPH through city streets. Many times, the guy has no idea it's there and slows down.

Your 5-year-old kid getting pushed down by another 5-year-old kid IS NOT a police matter. Talk to the other kid's parents.

If your kid won't do his homework or his chores, 911 is not the answer for a uniformed second-string parent.

If you hit your spouse in front of your children, your children will hit their spouse in front of their children.

If you rob a gas station, you're only going to get $20 but I get to see a K-9 dog use your arm as a chew toy. For all I care, you can keep the $20.

In one week of patrol work, in a large city, only about 10 minutes would be cool enough to be on the television show, COPS. If COPS was about report writing and accident reports; each show would be a week long.

Every traffic stop could end in gunfire, but we have to be polite and professional until that time.

I've taken about the same amount of men as women to jail for domestic violence, so NO it's not always the man.

Attention Victims: I need to know the WHO, WHAT, WHERE, WHEN, and HOW, not what meds you're on or what your 15 cats have peed on either.

Some cops don't like to be called cops, but I don't know why. Most don't care; we've been called worse.

If you find crack pipes in the lady's purse, there is a good chance they belong to her.

Cops know you pay taxes and that your taxes pay cops' salaries. Cops also pay taxes, which also pay cops' salaries, so, hey, this traffic stop is on me! Now sign here and press hard.

Now a variation on the above for the irate offender: You say, "my tax money pays your salary, so you work for me!" LEO: I pay taxes too, so I figure I'm self-employed.

When you see an officer walk into the room, a polite greeting of "hello, how are you" is much more appropriate than, "Uh-Oh Jim, it looks like they're here for you!" Hold back from putting your arms up and exclaiming, "I didn't do it!" It will surely save you from looking like an unoriginal horse's ass.

If there are police cars, fire trucks, or ambulances at your neighbor's house then there is a problem. You don't need to meddle into your neighbor's business by asking us what's happening. Your curiosity, no matter how strong, is not a reason to violate your neighbor's privacy. If it's something that YOU need to worry about, we would've knocked on your door and told you.

Remember that you and I enjoy the benefits of Constitutional rights; so, does the guy you suspect of stealing your stuff. No, I can't go search his house for your property just because you suspect he might be involved.

No, I don't know your cousin who's a police officer in (fill in location anywhere in the US). We Don't All Know Each Other!

No, your crappy band doesn't have until 10:00 pm to blast your crappy music out of that garage.

If I can see a 12-year-old in your house finishing a beer bong I don't need a warrant.

If you don't know what the speed limit is what makes you think it's 65 MPH.

If a neighborhood association asks for police to start ticketing in their neighborhood, one of the first five ticketed is on the board of the association.

When you're blocking an area to traffic (both foot and vehicle), "No, you can't go that way" doesn't mean, "You're special, so by all means, go ahead."

If an officer is standing in front of you with his hand outstretched, waving furiously at you, plus he's yelling for you to "Stop", it's usually a good idea to do as he asks. Please don't keep driving towards the officer.
Flares + cruiser parked at an angle = a place you can't go, even if it's a ramp to the interstate.

Don't run from the police and then attempt to hide in a warehouse. Especially don't do this if the officers tell you that the dog is going to be let loose, as this will generally result in the dog winning. They leave some pretty marks, by the way.

"Stop resisting" means EXACTLY THAT; don't say "I'm not resisting" as you throw a punch at the officer's face.

Just because you're handcuffed doesn't mean you won't go on the ground if you attempt to assault an officer. We don't even make exceptions for pregnant women who bite us, either.

Did you really think I wasn't going to find that large lump of crack you got clenched in your butt? It's either the world's largest 'roid, or you got something you ain't supposed to have.

If you tell us you borrowed the jacket from a friend, just before we search it, we know you have something and it's still gonna be the jacket.

Officers don't know why, for some reason, you think we will believe it when you tell us that you don't know how it got there. (see above)

Stopping a green man in a blue shirt and pink pants a block away from an armed robbery when the suspect description is a green man in a blue shirt and pink pants IS NOT racial profiling.

Just because you have your hazard lights on, doesn't mean it is okay to park in the fire lane and run into the store; even if you really need milk!

No, I will not go get your 6-year-old from their friend's house because it is 1:00am and you don't want to drive 3 minutes. Maybe you should set a curfew and enforce it. I am not a bad police officer; you're a bad parent.

Don't call us and ask us to solve a problem in 10 minutes that took 2 years to create.

And last but not least: 99% of Police Officers do their job honestly and with great pride, we try to do our job well. Often, we have to work in environments where we are the only ones that have to follow the rules. A veteran Sergeant told me on my first day of patrol, when you wear that uniform everything you do is a liability. We do make mistakes and due to the nature of the job sometimes they have horrible results. Sometimes minor mistakes cost police officers their lives, at a rate of 1 of every 50 hours.

Vest Up!
Stay Safe!

And THANK YOU for All That You Do!

ABOUT THE AUTHOR

Charlotte Hopkins is a freelance writer from Pittsburgh, Pennsylvania. Her writing has been published in a variety of newspapers, magazines and websites. She was published in Chicken Soup for the Soul, Shadows & Light Anthology, and Authors for Haiti.

She wrote feature pieces for Newscastic.com, highlighting life and times of Pittsburgh. Her article, 5 More Minutes, was a tribute to lives lost on September 11th. In 2005, it was read in a military service for soldiers and their families. She released the first three books in her "365 Days" book series.

They are titled:

365 Days of Writing Fiction

365 Days of Writing Nonfiction

365 Days of Family Fun

She is currently a reporter for the South Hills Messenger Newspaper and the Mon Valley Independent. Along with her writing, Charlotte was a Preschool Teacher and Activity Coordinator for more than 10 years. The work she is most proud of is being a mother of two up-and-coming authors.

Other titles from Higher Ground Books & Media:

Wise Up to Rise Up by Rebecca Benston

A Path to Shalom by Steen Burke

From a Hole in My Life to a Life Made Whole by Janet Kay Teresa

Overcomer by Forrest Henslee

Miracles: I Love Them by Forest Godin

32 Days with Christ's Passion by Mark Etter

The Magic Egg by Linda Phillipson

The Tin Can Gang by Chuck David

Whobert the Owl by Mya C. Benston

Dear You by Derra Nicole Sabo

For His Eyes Only by John Salmon, PhD

Add these titles to your collection today!

http://highergroundbooksandmedia.com

www.ingramcontent.com/pod-product-compliance
Lightning Source LLC
LaVergne TN
LVHW011345080426
835511LV00005B/127